What people are saying about *THE ARTFUL LIAR*:

"In THE ARTFUL LIAR, Cynthia Friedlander has given us the compelling story of a decade-long relationship between a charming sociopathic liar and the successful, talented and intelligent woman who loves him. When she at last discovers – and can no longer explain away or deny – the extent of his lies, she must learn to fight to regain her self-respect, self-esteem, and her very existence. THE ARTFUL LIAR ultimately becomes a heart-wrenching cautionary tale for modern, urban women of all ages."
Pat Carr, author of *ONE PAGE AT A TIME*

"Cynthia Friedlander's THE ARTFUL LIAR delves into the story of a betrayed woman with such depth and honesty, one can almost feel her pain as she becomes aware of the extent of her betrayer's lies. She must come to terms with the knowledge that a man she loved and shared her life with had deceived her for years, and Friedlander pours her soul into her writing of the woman's pain and, eventual healing. Friedlander provides a service to the many people who will find comfort in seeing themselves and their stories reflected in this book."
Ellen Schnier, LCSW, Psychotherapist

"What a beautiful and graceful telling of an extraordinary story. I could not stop turning the pages and anticipating what would happen next - what great storytelling is all about. Surely this book is going to touch many lives. So many of us have been deceived by one(s) we loved; this retelling of how the author overcame, regained her confidence, and moved on was what really made the book for me. I am also very impressed with the guiding messages. Such a gift for anyone who is in the valley and trying to climb back up the mountain."
Elise Davis-McFarland, PhD, former VP, Trident Technical College
Certified Speech-Language Pathologist

"Thank you for giving us THE ARTFUL LIAR. This book stirred my emotions and interest at all times. I could feel pain and anger. What a strong and courageous woman. THE ARTFUL LIAR will help many women who have found themselves in a deceptive relationship."
Florence Schmelzer, Native New Yorker, Relationship Survivor,
Former Manager, New York Convention and Visitors Bureau

Also by Cynthia Leeds Friedlander

Speak Easy: The Communication Guide for Career and Life Success

Breastless Intimacy: A Celebration of Love, Loss and Learning

Gagged: The 10 Mistakes That Stop Women From Being Heard At Work

On Butterfly Wings (Poetry)

The Artful Liar

Reflections on Betrayal and Deception

Cynthia Leeds Friedlander

*With
110 guiding messages
for reclaiming
and living your truth*

Published by
Hybrid Global Publishing
301 E 57th Street, 4th fl
New York, NY 10022

Copyright © 2018 by Cynthia Leeds Friedlander

All rights reserved. No part of this book may be reproduced or transmitted in any form or by any means, electronic or mechanical, including photocopying, recording, or by any information storage and retrieval system, without the written permission of the Publisher, except where permitted by law.

Manufactured in the United States of America, or in the United Kingdom when distributed elsewhere.

Friedlander, Cynthia
    The Artful Liar: Reflections on betrayal and deception
    LCCN: 2017961461
    ISBN: 978-1-938015-92-2
    eBook: 978-1-938015-93-9

Cover design: Joe Potter
Cover photo: Manjit Kaur
Copyediting: Claudia Volkman
Interior design: Claudia Volkman

TheArtfulLiar.com
TodaysEmpoweredWoman.com

The Artful Liar is one woman's fictionalized memoir written in the universal third-person female voice as a series of stand-alone vignettes based on the author's perspectives, experiences, and imagination. Individual identities, situations, and histories have been invented by the author. References to real people, events, establishments, or locales are intended to provide authenticity and have been used fictitiously. All characters and dialogue in *The Artful Liar* come from the author's imagination and are not to be construed as real or representative of any existing individuals.

To contact the author for workshop facilitation, coaching or speaking engagements:
TodaysEmpoweredWoman.com

To participate in a support forum for women who have been betrayed or deceived:
MenWhoLie.com

For Jay, who taught me the importance of accepting what is and the imperative of refraining from lies.

"The world breaks everyone and afterward many are **strong** at the **broken places**."
ERNEST HEMINGWAY, *A Farewell to Arms*

―――

"There are only two or three human stories, and they go on repeating themselves as fiercely as if they had never happened before."
WILLA CATHER, *Oh Pioneers*

CONTENTS

Love's Desire 1

AFTER MATTHEW
Worst Nightmare 5

BEFORE MATTHEW
Hide-n-Seek 13
Wasena Bridge 15
Vicarious Love 19
Life Lesson 23
Il Compidoglio 27
Living in Paradise 33
Panic's Embrace 39
Joyride 43
Saying Goodbye 49

MATTHEW
B.B. King's 55
Living Blind 61
Sanctuary 71
Balancing Act 81
Year of Bliss, Year of Pain 89

AFTER MATTHEW
Hindsight Is 20/20 119
Collusion with the Liar 127
Making Lists 137
Dirty Specifics/Big Lies/Small Travesties 151
Trusting Your Gut 173
Picking Up the Pieces: Reclaiming Hope 179
Sanctuary Lost and Found Within 189

Final Dream 199

Love's Desire
(The Response)

They were making love.

The curtains were fluttering from the wind gusts floating in through the open window. She heard the rain spattering on the corrugated patio awning below, as if the clatter were appreciative applause, bringing a slight giggle to her sensual satisfaction.

"I never want to do this with anyone else but you."

She searched deep into his eyes, waiting for a response . . .

but the man who wanted to be much more than he was, who wanted to be the center of her world, the man who proclaimed she was the love of his life, the ever-ready man who wrapped words around any situation in the flash of an instant – averted his eyes from her gaze . . .

and said nothing.

After Matthew

Worst Nightmare
(2014)

She knew one day she would look back and find lightness and be able to laugh about it all. She also knew it would take a great deal of healing for that to happen; it would take much thoughtful processing to gain enough understanding to find humor in this awful mess of deception; it would take time, lots and lots of time.

In the horrendous week of pain and tears following her discovery of Matthew's years of betrayal, she incessantly watched the clip of Louis C. K. declaring men as the biggest danger women face. He colorfully described men as the #1 most menacing deliverers of mayhem and injury to women while in contrast he pointed out how men face only heart disease as their biggest threat. Each time she watched the video, she would laugh franticly at Louis C.K. being admonished by his willful demonic male heart. "Dude, you can't keep doing this. I told you three strokes ago that this is not smart."

In her mind's eye she could see Matthew, who'd had three strokes in the last year, leaning back against the headboard of her bed with the sheet pulled up to his armpits, vigorously rubbing the top of his forehead. It was as if he believed his desperate scalp-rubbing could compel the version of the truth he was frantically trying to locate to the surface to be able to force out an answer when she asked for openness. She could hear him clearing his throat in nervous desperation, like a shrieking cornered bull in a bull ring, terrified to have to fight publicly against a bigger foe than could ever be matched or conquered. She could recognize all the head-rubbing and throat-clearing over the years as obvious indicators of Matthew's desperate struggle to find some version of "his truth" to offer her, to satisfy her.

With all the incriminating evidence she'd just uncovered, she could look back and realize how artful he'd always been at deception, at withholding, at invention, at fabrication ... at lying. She finally and clearly saw how lying was an art form for Matthew, how the contemptful judgment she'd held against him all those years (and had labeled her conclusions as harsh and unkind) had been well-founded, and how the renewed love, acceptance and understanding she'd given him the past year had been fool-hearted and certainly unmerited.

That last time they were together, a couple months before the discovery of Matthew's deception, she'd pleaded for open communication and truth, never suspecting the existence of anything as sordid and hurtful as the years of deceit she'd just found out.

They were in bed, where they always had their serious deep talks, where they shared the innermost corners of their souls ... or so she'd believed. They'd just watched *Now Voyager*, her favorite old black-and-white movie from 1942. Charlotte (Bette Davis) had said to her married lover, "Oh, Jerry, don't let's ask for the moon. We've got the stars."

She could hear the clock ticking next to the bed, like a night watchman constantly announcing the futility of longing. They'd taken a bubble bath together, a revived intimacy from early in their relationship, that had fallen away from their treasured rituals. Matthew had complained of back pain, withdrawing the delightful pressure of his fingers, leaving her alone in the bubbles, surrounded by the many deliciously scented candles she'd lit. She'd hung the soaking-wet, thick washcloth over the shower rod; she'd used it to cover the top of her chest and neck to keep from getting chilled as she leaned back between Matthew's legs with her back against his chest in her ancient accommodating bathtub. The cloth was still dripping into the remaining bath water, joining the percussion of the clock.

She'd been pleading for him to open up and share his pain and deepest feelings. "I can't keep on doing this if you're so closed off. You keep saying the words will come. I'm feeling more and more like the OTHER woman in your life, not the woman you say you're in love with. It's as if you're somewhere else. I can see and touch you; I just can't feel your presence."

She'd noticed the dark rough growth embedded in his scalp as he vigorously rubbed his head. She knew as soon as she saw it, more than likely it was melanoma. It was burnt and crusty in appearance and looked like a piece of Bibi's dog kibble stuck in Matthew's scalp. She'd intended to say something about it but their heavy and frustrating one-way conversation distracted her from mentioning it and afterwards she forgot all about it.

Weeks later, at the very moment she stumbled into his extensive and long-standing web of deception, he emailed her he'd been in the ER at the hospital with a massive migraine and blurred vision — probably a precursor to another stroke — and they'd told him they noticed a small brown spot on the top of his head that looked suspicious and were sending him to get a biopsy. As she read his desperate frightened email, her thoughts traveled back to the abandoned bubble bath and empty lovemaking, and then locked on the forgotten dark malignancy she'd observed blazing from the top of his head like a Scarlet Letter proclaiming his guilt.

After all, she'd agreed to be hidden in his life the past year. She'd come crawling back full of Acceptance, Apology and Appreciation. When she asked him to take her back, nine months after they'd broken up, he revealed he was in a new relationship with a woman who'd just been diagnosed with a serious potentially life-threatening/inoperable tumor. He spoke of the biopsy surgery scheduled in ten days. He said, "This woman loves me the way I always loved you. I won't abandon her in the middle of this crisis."

She felt the dagger of jealousy and regret stab her heart as she recognized all she'd withheld from Matthew for so long. They'd been a bi-coastal, long-distance couple for almost eleven years and she'd told him it was over in a way Matthew found reprehensible. She'd broken up with him in a letter attached to an email.

It was a tender loving letter she'd composed with great care. She'd prepared him, telling him she'd written something important he should read in privacy and solitude. She'd held her breath for several seconds before she'd finally hit "SEND" and it was done.

Matthew,

This is very hard to write. I want to tell you all that's in my heart.

I want to start with how much I've loved you and how wonderful you are. You've been steadfast and adoring. You've been generous and loving. You've been attentive and supportive. You've been understanding and accepting. You've always been there for me throughout many challenging milestones and passages.

We've shared major life events that have been both bonding and destructive. We've loved one another deeply yet differently. There's been an imbalance between our feelings for each other we've both accepted and lived with. Our feelings have grown and deepened for ten years. Our lives have been intertwined and we've been family to each other.

I've been faithful to you and have been accepting of what we have together. I've not been looking for more. I've felt safe inside my cocoon. I've wanted to protect my heart. I've felt sheltered. I've felt insulated. I've felt finished, like it's done and over.

Quite unexpected and unsought, all that has changed. I've had a response to a man I've known my entire life yet never known in any personal way or even spoken to before now. I've told him I've been in a relationship for ten years with someone I care about and love. My feelings for him are surprising, strong, and clear.

I want to move forward without being duplicitous or hiding. I don't want to do anything behind your back. I don't want to cheat on you. I want to be honest. I want to be able to find a way not to hurt you. You've always said you want me to have more. You've always said you want me to be with someone who can provide for me in ways you cannot.

I hope, at some point, you can be happy for me and I hope you can be free to find someone who will love you the way you want to be

> loved. You've always told me I haven't loved you the way you want to be loved. You've always told me you know I'm not in love with you. You've told me you've been examining moving on so you could have a complete relationship with someone.
>
> I'm thinking of Chuck's lyrics, being each other's angels and meeting when it's time. You've been an angel for me for so long and I cherish that with all my heart.
>
> I care about you so much, Matthew, and always will.

She'd thought they would talk. She'd wanted to talk. His reaction was volatile and his anger was extreme; he'd adamantly refused to speak with her and because of his intense rage she declined to read anything he sent after the first two mean-spirited explosive email responses from him. And it had ended. She'd terminated their relationship because she'd met someone and didn't want even to kiss this man behind Matthew's back; she never wanted to cheat on him; she never wanted to be in an intimate relationship with more than one person or to be in a relationship with someone who was in an intimate relationship with someone else.

Early on, soon after they first met, she'd asked him for two promises: "You have to promise me if you leave your wife, it won't be because of me. You can't leave Tina for me. I can't be the reason you're leaving your marriage."

"And you have to swear to me you'll never lie to Tina, to me or to anyone else."

He gave both promises without a moment's hesitation and added a third. "I also promise I won't fall in love with you while I'm still married to Tina."

"You can't promise not to fall in love. You can't promise something like that! I'm only asking you to keep the promises I asked for."

Twelve years later, one year after they'd reconnected, she inadvertently opened Pandora's Box and all the lies and deception tumbled out like the worst nightmare imaginable.

LETTING GO MESSAGES

WORST NIGHTMARE

She learned how important it is to:

- Give yourself time to heal when you're going through tough times.

- Pay attention to the signs along the way.

- Hold tightly to your core values and beliefs.

- Refuse to be in any relationship that requires your being hidden.

- Recognize how deception is always wrong even when the intent is protective.

Before Matthew

Hide-n-Seek
(1950)

It was hard to breathe with her head under the plump soft sofa cushion but she thought she'd found the perfect hiding place this time. It was too scary concealing herself somewhere way off in the recesses of the vast new house.

Her big sister and cousin were much older and they would often leave her hiding in the deep dark coat closet and go off and forget about her altogether. She'd be sitting in the light-starved bathtub when they'd sneak up on her very quietly and scream a big terrifying "BOO!" yanking back the rattling shower curtain with the giant blood red roses.

Yes, this was definitely better, right out in the open, in the middle of the sun-filled living room.

"We can see you, you know! That's not really hiding!"

Their howling mocking cries and laughter were ringing in her ears when she proclaimed, "You can't see me 'cause I can't see you."

Let them think she was just a silly little four-year-old. She knew how terrifying it felt when she was in those real hiding places waiting for them to come find her alone in the dark.

She made her choice to hide in full view this time with her head under the pillow, knowing exactly how to keep from being frightened or feeling abandoned.

LETTING GO MESSAGES

HIDE-N-SEEK

She learned how important it is to:

- Look for creative ways to deal with fear.

- Diminish intimidators by seeing yourself as competent and confident.

- Expand your perspective so you can enhance your beliefs and actions.

- Find ways to change the playing field to give yourself equal footing with foes.

- Remain true to your own viewpoint even in the face of ridicule.

Wasena Bridge
(1953)

The first thing she'd clung to in childhood was childhood. She knew and thought about how protected her life was. She was wiser, more serious, and more mature than other children her age. As a little girl, she somehow sensed the burdens and responsibilities of growing up and wanted to bask in the adoration and safety she experienced as the good-girl daughter in her family. She was seven years younger than her sister and experienced life more like an only child than as the second of two siblings.

At the early age of seven, she was allowed to take public transportation all by herself after school to go "to work" at the store her parents owned downtown. Every time she rode the city bus back home alone, crossing the Wasena Bridge, she would feel this deep awareness of what being alive meant and of the ultimate terrifying outcome of aging. She would feel herself breathe, with an intense desire to hold onto every moment and stop time, knowing each breath she took was another step closer to her last. She wanted to be able to stop breathing to stay a child forever; she wanted to cheat death.

She'd been only four years old when she woke up terrified. She'd just drifted off to sleep into the beginning of a dream where the little brindle bunny her sister had found near the curb and buried that afternoon had jumped onto her bed and asked her to come out to play with him. She was so happy to see the bunny hopping across her bed when suddenly he collapsed in a big, wet, red puddle like the one her sister had found him in earlier. In her dream, she saw her sister pick him up and go to the back of their yard to the shed where the shovel was stored. Her big sister started digging a second hole to put the lifeless bunny into and each time she dug a hole for the curled-up bunny, another bunny would appear, ask her to play, and then flop into another red pool of liquid. She woke up frightened and screeching, as she put together the end of life for the bunny with the end of her own life. Her horrifying thoughts of the unacceptability of annihilation propelled her from her bed and she flew down the stairs in her pink and white nightgown into her mother's arms, sobbing from her fear, oblivious to the room full of guests who were visiting in her home with her parents. Her mother spoke soothing words to calm her back to bed.

"Sweetie, you don't have to be afraid of dying. You're a little girl who is well and safe. People die when they're very old and very sick. You must think of your happy home with everyone here who loves you and will always protect you from bad things."

From then on, she added these supplications to the end of her nightly "Dear God" prayer, just before "Amen":

"Don't let me think of bad things. Don't let me have bad dreams. And please let me die in my sleep."

She would continue to believe in Santa Claus for a few more years and her blind leap of faith into the hands of God would endure through high school but that night of death's terror would seal her maturity and suspicion of magic forever.

When she was nine years old, she saw Mary Martin in the role of Peter Pan on television. Watching it enthralled her and left her floating, *knowing* she could fly. She traveled in dreams to soar on high, awaking with a sense of flight that felt more real than the bed she slept and dreamt in.

Her fear of airplane flight arrived simultaneously or perhaps had always been there in some innate form. And so it was that her death fright and desire to stay a child forever were tightly bundled and the Peter Pan anthem, "I Won't Grow Up" (written by Mark Charlap), became intertwined with her fundamental little girl soul.

Her youthful exuberance would always be nourished, growing into a maturity that set her apart, giving her a magnetism that would always draw people to her.

LETTING GO MESSAGES

WASENA BRIDGE

She learned how important it is to:

- Appreciate the gifts of life you receive.

- Accept the realities of existence we all face.

- Make every day have meaning by soaring as high as you can.

- Take in the simple wonders that surround you.

- Let go of worries you cannot change.

VICARIOUS LOVE
(1957)

They were in the car. Her mother was driving her home from a party. Her mother had just taught her the meaning of the word "vicarious" and she could feel herself being sucked away; it was becoming hard to breathe. Teaching her this definition was meant to be the ultimate accolade; yet she instinctively felt this word "vicarious" was stifling and invasive ... a burden actually, rather than the declaration of love as proclaimed,

"You're so special and gifted; you can achieve all the things I missed out on and I can experience them through you."

All the failed achievements of her mother's life had suddenly been transformed into her challenges and measurements of worthiness.

In the same breath, her mother described the difference between liking and loving, and told her how liking was a much higher standard of affection. "You *have* to love your daughters; that's just a given." her mother said, "but you don't have to like them."

Her mother made it clear that "liking" was withheld from her bad-girl older sister, reinforcing once again the good-girl/bad-girl roles in their family. "I like you; I don't like your sister."

It would be like that throughout her life, her mother experiencing life through whatever she was doing and choosing: her losses and gains, her friends and relationships, her interests and passions.

When she was in her thirties, going through divorce, her mother said, "There's no way I can go with your father and enjoy this beautiful trip to Europe with you being so miserably unhappy."

These types of comments over the years were often accompanied by "I can't help it; I'm your mother; that's the way a mother is supposed to feel."

Having heard those words with such frequency over time, she would often search in vain to find those same feelings later in her own experience as a mother. When her son was ten months old, she and Hank traveled to Italy with him to visit Hank's father. The baby had stayed awake for seventeen of the twenty hours of travel via airplane flights and train rides to get to Forte dei Marmi on the Tuscan Riviera.

Within a few days after their arrival, the baby got a severe cold and a doctor was summoned. Seeing her little son sick and in discomfort in a foreign country far from home was very difficult and unsettling. With Hank in the next room to watch over their sick baby finally down for a nap, she walked up the steep hill behind their hotel room to take in the magnificent vista of the coastline, to feel the breeze on her cheeks, and almost bumped into her father-in-law at the crest of the knoll. He smilingly inquired in French, their only common language, "You wish you were the one who's sick, n'est-ce pas? You want to take his illness and make it yours so he won't be suffering, oui?"

She didn't want or wish any of that. These thoughts never crossed her mind. She simply wanted her son to be well. She looked at the grandfather in disbelief and responded, "Non, pas du tout. I just wish he would get well fast and not be sick."

Her son would be a grown man when she eventually put the question her father-in-law asked her during that trip to Italy together with her mother's teaching her the word "vicarious" in the car on the way to a party when she was in the fifth grade.

It was a have-your-cake-and-eat-it type of Friday night. Her mother was driving her to a birthday party at the house of Teddy Harrison, the most popular boy in her class. She'd just been asked to be on television the next day for a local

Saturday morning children's program called *Maxine's Corner*. "We've got an emergency and we need your help right away. We need you to fill in for Amy Levin."

The little girl who was a regular on the show had come down with chicken pox and was not going to be able to be there. Most of televised programming was live in those days. She would have to memorize the entire script that night in preparation for the next day on television. There would be no time for rehearsal or practice.

On that party night in the car with her mother – when she learned the meaning of "vicarious" - she was only eleven years old. What a big responsibility for a fifth grader! What expectations and demands she would carry through life!

The thought of missing the last party of the school year, felt like the end of the world. She wanted both, to be there for the party and to stay up late afterwards to learn her lines.

"Please, please let me go to the party. I'll come home early. I don't have to stay until the end. It's the last party before school lets out next week. I just HAVE to be there. Please, please! I can memorize my lines when I come home. I know I can. You can help me learn my lines. Please, please say yes and let me go."

She'd convinced her mother to agree to her plan, to take her to the party and to bring her home a little early and then to stay up late to help her memorize the script she was required to know in the morning.

Her imagined far-from-real-life beliefs were reinforced that night and on many subsequent occasions: she could get what she wanted without giving up anything; she could have it all, have her cake and eat it too; she was loved and liked; she was the good girl; she was a star.

Letting Go Messages

Vicarious Love

She learned how important it is to:

- Know there is nothing you can do to make someone else's life whole.

- Choose your goals in life for yourself rather than to please someone else.

- Stand up for your beliefs respectfully even in the face of challenge.

- Give unconditionally to those you love without expectation or demand for reciprocation.

- Raise the bar and reach for more by stretching beyond what you think you can achieve.

Life Lesson
(1958)

She'd always been confident and comfortable with her identity and religious heritage. She'd always felt acceptance and love reinforced throughout her childhood.

Even when the little Verela girl from her second-grade class was visiting across the street and was craftily coached and coerced by the nasty older cousin who lived there to run out into the front yard and yell across the road, "I'm not going to play with you, you Dirty Little Jew!" she'd handled that verbal assault easily with her sharp, ever-ready, seven-year-old tongue.

She'd shouted back, standing on the edge of the stone wall that lined her front yard with her tiny hands cupped to her mouth, "Well, I'm not going to play with YOU, you Dirty Little Greek!"

Both young girls liked each other warmly and would have happily been playmates that day. It was just an event of ignorant childhood goading instigated by a mean older bully and the resulting proud fast defense it prompted.

That evening when her mother came home, the beloved housekeeper had said, "I know you would've wanted me to reprimand her for that kind of hate language, but I was so proud of her quick response, I just couldn't do it."

She didn't like being singled out for being different, for being Jewish, yet quickly and effortlessly came to her own defense when attacked.

Favoritism was as uncomfortable for her as derision. She squirmed behind her desk when her first-grade teacher, who was a close friend of the family, gave

Lindsey Holmes and her each an individual box of big fat Crayola crayons on the first day of school. She didn't like being singled out with Lindsay, because they were pretty girls, because they were special girls, making the rest of the class wait until the second day of school to get their own crayon boxes.

The summer when she was twelve, she went to sleep-away camp in Abingdon, Virginia for seven weeks. She'd been to sleep-away camp the prior two summers but for only two weeks each time. This was big girl camp with serious living away from home for almost two months.

There was a beautiful girl in her cabin with inky black silken hair named Miranda who came from Mississippi. One warm afternoon following a torrential cloudburst when a few of the girls were in the bunk for some rest-period breaktime from their busy activity schedules, she was sitting on the end of Miranda's bed, engrossed in conversation with Miranda about boys while Miranda was simultaneously writing a letter home to her brother.

Miranda was talking about her wonderful older brother Tom and pulled out a picture of him from her red leather wallet with black lacing along the edges and announced,

"Tom's really handsome. This isn't a good picture of him though. It makes him look like a Jew."

Stunned and deeply hurt by Miranda's words, she backed away from the bed and out of the cabin with tears starting to stream down her cheeks. She ran next door to her cousin Lonnie's cabin and burst into uncontrollable sobs.

"What's wrong? Are you homesick?"

She shook her head, getting out the words, "No, no! NO!"

She could barely talk or breathe to tell her cousin what had just happened; she was so hurt. Together she and Lonnie walked up the hill to the big log house with the window boxes streaming with purple petunia and salmon pink geranium blossoms where Miss Penny, the Camp Director, lived.

Life Lesson

The valuable Life Lesson that came from that painful experience was priceless and would stay with her forever. Miss Penny talked to her in such an embracing, significant, and supportive way. She hugged her warmly and provided words of comfort and healing by saying over and over in many different ways how the Jews were God's Chosen People and because she was Jewish how special that made her. Miss Penny also told her about the necessary suffering that comes with being chosen.

"Don't you know because you're Jewish, no one can ever take away how extraordinary you are, no matter how harsh or mean the words are that attempt to tear you down."

She and Lonnie walked out into the afternoon dappled sunlight filtering through the trees and she felt a surge of inner strength and healing freedom from the piercing wound that had ripped through her heart less than an hour before.

Letting Go Messages

Life Lesson

She learned how important it is to:

- Believe in who you are.

- Minimize disdainful attacks by standing up for yourself.

- Be strong in the face of derision.

- Remember: People who attack you are usually ignorant and often insecure.

- Know your own strengths so no one can diminish you through verbal assault.

Il Compidoglio
(1968)

It was the last semester of her senior year. She was studying at The University of Grenoble. She'd declared French as her new (third change) major at the end of the first semester of her junior year and it had been too late for the traditional junior year abroad program all foreign language majors participated in. When Hank phoned her in Grenoble from New York and asked her what she wanted for her birthday, which was the day he would arrive in France two weeks and three days later at the beginning of her Spring break, she replied, "You know."

Hank immediately understood. "We can't get married like that without our families and a real engagement and a wedding planned. Our mothers would be devastated."

He called her again two nights later to tell her he'd just had dinner with her mother in New York at Bill Hong's Chinese Restaurant on West 56th Street. She could feel herself stop breathing for several seconds as she heard him say, "Your mother said she thinks this is too beautiful a trip we've got planned. She thinks it should be our honeymoon. I asked her if she really meant that and she said yes. Here, I'll put your mother on the phone so you can speak with her."

And just like that, they were engaged. Seventeen days later, they were married in Rome; without a family member present or a previously known friend as witness.

The day after Hank's second call, she'd spent most of the afternoon inquiring about getting married in Grenoble. She'd learned there was a six-week waiting period in France required to "post the banns" which resulted in their deciding to get married in Italy where there was no required waiting period for the marriages of foreigners. They were going to travel to Milan anyway for her to meet Hank's father, Jacob, who lived there so the plan quickly changed to a wedding in Milan.

She took the bus from Grenoble to Lyons to meet Hank's plane on April 5th, 1968. The smoke was thick and the body odor strong. She loved the pungent smell of the unfiltered Gauloises cigarettes, with their dark Turkish tobacco, and the unbathed, un-deoderanted armpits of the men; the combination was earthy and sensual and so, so French.

She struggled to hear the radio announcements coming from the speakers in the ceiling of the bus. It was hard to make out the announcer's words because of the road and wind noise coming through the open windows, the various conversations around her, and the interrupted, static-filled broadcast. She could make out that Martin Luther King, Jr. had been murdered in Memphis hours earlier. She shuddered in sadness as she made sure she'd understood the shocking news correctly. It sounded like the entire United States was in full riot.

Arriving at the airport in Lyons with ample extra time, she settled into the waiting area, checking the time incessantly. Flight 776 from Paris arrived and the passengers disembarked. Hank did not get off of the designated flight. Her requests for information and verification of the passenger list and flight schedules from the Air France counter representative were frustrating and fruitless, in spite of her fluency in French. Every response was the same no matter how many different questions she asked. "En principe, your fiancé should have been on Flight 776." Well, in principe or not, he wasn't on Flight 776. She knew at some point, if he didn't arrive, she would have to get back on a bus and travel the forty kilometers back to Grenoble.

She told herself, en principe, Hank would have to arrive eventually. She was beyond worried; she was scared. Maybe New York City was in flames. Maybe no planes were leaving the U.S. because of the assassination. She had to calm her mind from these kinds of thoughts. En principe, he would get there. Another two hours passed before the next flight from Paris landed at the Aéroport Alpes–Isère. She'd never been so happy to see someone walk down the ramp stairs of an airplane. Hank's flight from New York to Paris had arrived late and he'd missed his connection to Lyons. En principe, she thought, Air France should surely have had that information.

It turned out there was an official postage-type stamp required for their marriage certificate and the stamp was only available in Rome and would take many days for its arrival in Milan. They kissed Jacob goodbye and drove from Milan to Rome where, on an elevator asking for information, they met a Signore Bigini who was a magistrate in charge of the death certificate office. Hank explained their challenge and Signore Bigini was ecstatic to help them find and obtain the needed stamp for their marriage document and also spontaneously and graciously arranged for them to have two witnesses and a photographer for their wedding.

Civil marriage ceremonies in Rome take place in Il Compidoglio. She had bought a beautiful white crepe mini-dress in Grenoble that had quite a bridal feel to it with long bell sleeves and two dozen cloth-covered buttons down the front with fabric button-loop closings rather than button holes. It was an elegant dress and she wondered if she and Hank were going to be married in some utilitarian bureaucratic office space where her dress might be rather out of place.

Hank had brought her a beautiful lace mantilla sent from her mother to wear as a wedding veil. Il Compidoglio turned out to be a regal space with grand historic ambiance. The walls were covered in formal rich red brocade and she and Hank were seated in throne-like gilded chairs with red velvet upholstery for the ceremony. The photograph in their Star City newspaper wedding announcement would have a dramatic aura and look as if she and Hank were royalty.

After the wedding, as she and Hank walked down the stairs along the side of the grand marble Victor Emmanual Monument on their way to the Piazza Venezia, with young school girls squealing congratulatory "Auguri!" to them, she felt ominously terrified. She'd just gotten married in a country where there was no divorce. Her fear this marriage was an irreparable mistake fed right into the impossibility of Italian divorce, without her making the obvious connection to the Catholic Church, the actual basis for why Italians couldn't be divorced.

On her wedding day in Rome, her terror far outweighed her joy. Her gut told her something essential was missing. She silently and secretly repeated her beliefs inside her head:

> "Hank is the handsome Jewish 'perfect provider' I'm 'supposed' to marry."

> "I'm about to graduate from college and the thought of being on my own and supporting myself is completely inconceivable, exceedingly horrifying, and quite unacceptable."

> "Jodie took three years after graduating from college to find a husband and it nearly destroyed Mother. I can't be the second daughter to bring her that kind of pain."

> "My delicious adored non-Jewish best-playmate boyfriend, Harry, has discovered he's gay and is off somewhere in Morocco with his new friends who're much better suited to him than I am."

> "And just like Mother wants me to believe, it would be immoral for me to be traveling and sleeping with a man I'm not married to. After all, I'm a GOOD GIRL."

There was no crystal ball there that April wedding day to see into her future to inform her she would eventually fall madly in love with her gorgeous husband who spoke five languages and who would be a devoted husband and father. She would have no way to know the very pedestal she so wanted to be on, that day in Rome when she married Hank, would at some point begin to feel like a bejeweled trap holding her prisoner and keeping her from finding her own strength and voice. She couldn't possibly have imagined that day when she first wore the wedding band she intended to keep on her finger for the rest of her life that she would venture outside of her marriage to find deep connection. She had no way to envision when those darling Italian schoolgirls cheered her wedding that eleven years later Hank would leave her for Mona.

That day in Rome, she had no way to imagine how much pain and loss and then learning and self-sufficiency would come from the dissolution of her Italian Il Compidoglio wedding … from her fated divorce from Hank.

Letting Go Messages

Il Compidoglio

She learned how important it is to:

- Refrain from making choices based in fear.

- Honor your commitments through honesty.

- Rely on yourself to provide your sense of well-being.

- Recognize every choice you make has repercussions.

- Examine the basis for your decisions and your doubts.

Living in Paradise
(1976)

Hank came home from work one night and announced at dinner he was being assigned to the Bahamas to set up a new off-shore bank. "How'd you like to live in Nassau for three to six months?"

She knew it must have unfolded slightly differently right after Hank asked that question but her vivid memory was she'd immediately gotten up from the table without providing a word in response and walked upstairs to their bedroom and started packing.

Their time in Nassau actually turned into eighteen months of living in Paradise. Initially they lived in a suite on the eighth floor of The Britannia Beach Hotel. They had a balcony that wrapped around the living room and master bedroom looking out past the beach with Caribbean turquoise sea meeting the sky at the horizon. Below, the canopy of gnarly pine trees with pinecones smaller than grapes hid the path to the beach. The recluse, Howard Hughes, lived on the entire ninth floor. No one had seen him leave his guarded, penthouse hideaway for years.

Their second home on Paradise Island was The Ocean Break Villas. Their two-bedroom condo had an enclosed courtyard with luscious bougainvillea growing up the fencing and hibiscus in profusion. Passing the night-blooming jasmine at the gate on the way to dinner in the evening was intoxicating. The tiny lizards scampered everywhere and the hermit crabs dragged their shells along the patio stones. She later joked about how pure and clean their life there was, saying, "We bathed but we didn't have to."

She spent hours on the beach collecting shells and floating in the warm and gentle, pale aqua, Mother Sea. She played tennis every day and soaked up the warmth of the sun, fully appreciating the gift of living in such a haven.

It was an idyllic life with her husband and little son and she'd never been happier or more content. When a friend and neighbor said to her in the swimming pool with their toddlers one day, "Oh, hon, you're so lucky!" she gloated internally, knowing deep in her core how true it was.

What she didn't know was that the consciousness-raising and new awareness she would gain during these days of perfection in Nassau, would completely destroy the treasured and protected life she was living.

She devoured several books a week, discovering diverse authors from Nabokov and Virginia Woolf to Tom Robbins. She would often later claim *Even Cowgirls Get the Blues* irreversibly changed her life. She read as if her brain had been forever starved for withheld words. With every book she read, she felt an awakening from her small-town isolation and then married oblivion. She recognized that the Civil Rights and Women's Movements had passed her by and suddenly, through all her reading and new awareness of how much she'd missed, she could feel her world and how she would live her life morphing into completely reconstructed entities with totally different operating platforms.

Her appreciation of the magnificence of the written word brought her to her early stabs at writing. It was enormously intimidating to appreciate the gifts of great writers and see her meager attempts to emulate them unfold in ink on blank paper, written by her own hand:

Irony Revealed - Nassau, Bahamas, Fall, 1976

Last night I dreamed about Harry again. The same dream but new. This time I told him, "I love you." and did not want nor need an answer. I awoke and sensed the difference in my dream and lay awake thinking, rethinking and finally knowing.

But often, lucid nocturnal visions fade by morning. That sense of knowing remains; yet the knowledge lies hidden somewhere in dawn's shadows…

Okay, gutless wonder! Big talker, lots of words, lots of opinions. Is it all empty rhetoric? Why should writing be so much harder? Is it simply because I have less practice at it or is it that nothing I say or think is worth committing to paper – to permanence?

Stare at the blank page long enough and something worthwhile will come to mind. Certainly, today has been out of the ordinary. Poor Elaine! (Poor me. Gutless wonder!) Honesty: the false front for cowardice:

It all began with those two dark hands coming over the gate. "Who's there? What do you want?" I shouted. Muffled responses. I asked again.

Elaine was already under the bed when I finally understood, "Immigration."

"I can't come out right now." I said, slamming and locking the doors and pulling the curtains.

Now what do I do? Poor Elaine, under the bed telling me to say I was "fearful for the child and the day-worker is not here today."

Gutless wonder responds, "I can't lie to them, Elaine. My husband and I could be sent to jail too, you know. They must know you're here. You can't hide under the bed this way."

The final cop-out, of course, is calling Hank to come home, please, now. *I venture into the yard again. "Madam why were you so rude before?"*

"I'm afraid of strangers." (meekly)

"But we identified ourselves. You were so rude."

"I didn't mean to be rude. Will you please wait here until my husband gets home?" (pleading)

I go back into the house and simultaneously try to appease and to ignore my little son J. He's beginning to get suspicious. Children do have this sixth sense when trouble is in the air. Elaine remains under the bed imploring me to go out and tell them that no one is here. Of course, I can't hear Elaine because J. is in high gear.

"Oh God, why isn't Hank home yet?" The minutes drip by like honey down the side of a jar – slow, sticky.

And he arrived and calmly handled all and poor Elaine was taken off to jail for being a Jamaican, for washing toilets, ironing shirts, loving a small boy, and on various occasions being surly, defiant and proud, while performing these and many other household duties and delights. But then, this is Nassau and there must be ten Bahamians unemployed for each one holding down a job, which may not even exist tomorrow. And so Jamaicans are not welcome here. And so Elaine will be sent away.

Hank: the center of my life.
my rock:
sensible, calm, responsible, reliable.
my friend:
funny, wise, loyal, fair.
my lover:
tender, passionate, gentle, unselfish.
Hank: my life

Thus is irony revealed. I write in search of self. I seek independence and direction. Maybe I even seek a merry-go-round's grab at that golden ring, Immortality. And, yes, I even write to proclaim the strength and glory of womanhood. How strange then, to begin with a dream of lost youth's faded love, an afternoon of weakness and inaction and an open admission of total devotion to and dependence on one man.

There in Nassau, without any awareness of what she was doing, she carefully planted the seeds for rebellious choices that resulted in the end of her contentment. It was as if she were breathing into a much deeper consciousness. Her life would come to feel like a circus act where her full and simple family life was expanded and then somehow exploded by the books she voraciously read while living in Nassau. It felt like all of the clowns had come out of the tiny car and she couldn't find any way to put them back inside or even understand how they'd ever fit in there to begin with. She was on some kind of trip to Oz except when she realized there was no place like home, home had been dismantled and no longer existed. She would have to find home inside herself. Going forward, she would have to create several versions of a new home before she could understand and accept, home is always within.

Letting Go Messages

Living in Paradise

She learned how important it is to:

- Find and follow your core expression and passion.

- Be open to new experiences, environments and cultures.

- Enrich your life through learning.

- Make connections between your actions and their impact on others.

- Live in the moment.

Panic's Embrace
(1979)

She'd gotten up very early that morning, just as the sun was rising. She couldn't sleep and knew she had to get out of the house, the big, 1793, almost empty, rambling two-story house they were using that summer. Hank's clients from Brazil had bought the historic landmark house, the massive barn on the water's edge, the three-acre pond and the seventeen acres of wooded land, half in Connecticut and half in Massachusetts. They told Hank he could use the property for his family until they were able to subdivide and resell their investment.

Her parents were still sleeping downstairs as was her five-year-old son in the next room. Hank was in the City. She'd awakened in an extreme panic, with a sickening dreadful awareness that her marriage was over. The reality of it had sunk in and brought her out of her morning dreams as if she'd inhaled a big stone that was weighing heavily on her heart, impeding her ability to breathe.

She threw on a pair of shorts and a t-shirt and dashed down the stairs and out the front door as quietly as she could to keep from waking her family. She knew she had to let it all out and couldn't risk revealing her weeping cries to her parents and her son. As she ran up the hill, shrieking, on the empty road in front of the house, the sun was exploding on the horizon, sparking and releasing her own emotional explosion. The reality of what she'd generated and the knowledge there was no way back to her sweet privileged, protected, provided-for life brought her to hysteria. How had she been so blind to the repercussions of her actions? How had she been so immune to what this would feel like?

She hadn't been at all prepared for this. The love and passion she'd risked her marriage for had seemed eternal and sure and so much more significant than what her marriage had become after eleven years … than what her marriage had ever been. It was as if the new relationship she'd sought had touched her in ways she'd never experienced before; she'd felt intertwined and connected at the soul. She would later call the dissolution of her marriage the result of latent adolescence. After all, she'd never rebelled the way most teenagers do. She would also say the reason her marriage came to an end was she had to get off the pedestal, she couldn't be the good girl any longer. When she started to come to her senses again, Hank had fallen in love with Mona and the marriage was destined to be over.

Running wildly up the hill and turning down the first street away from the house, all she could think of was how much she wanted her safe little world returned to her, and how sure she was that there was no longer any way back to it.

Out-of-control tears were streaming down her face and the sounds of her cries were agonizing. As she passed a path that led to a house she'd never noticed, an older woman came down the path and walked out into the road, wrapping her in a big hug and holding her until she'd finally exhausted her tears and sobbing.

She'd never seen the woman before and she would never see her again. The woman just held her and comforted her without words or judgment.

When she was calm and could breathe normally, the woman turned around and walked back up the path, disappearing without ever having spoken to her.

She slowly returned to the old house where her parents and child were sleeping, depleted of tears and spent of emotion, knowing she was forever changed, sensing she would always be ready to offer comfort and compassion to those in pain, and feeling she'd gained much through her loss in spite of the high price she'd paid.

Letting Go Messages

Panic's Embrace

She learned how important it is to:

- Pay attention as you go along.

- Be prepared for the outcomes you cultivate through each action you take.

- Realize every loss provides a lesson.

- Know the biggest learning comes from the biggest mistakes.

- Trust that comfort is always out there when you're in pain and hurting.

JOYRIDE
(2000)

She knew her life was better than a novel. She knew she had to write it. Words had always been her way out – her way in. She sat on the plane, smiling like a small child who'd observed a covert tryst between two hiding adults who thought of the child as a dog or cat, a pet who could never speak or tell what she'd just seen – but the child grinned, knowing more than the actors she'd witnessed. The flight was rough air choppy and her usual terror was nowhere. The smile took over as if she were it – one with the smile – one with the choppy air. Jostled, shaken around, senses tickled and invited to feel – invited to be.

Scrambling to find her pen – to be able to spread blue ink on flat white – it had been so long. The keyboard had become her word lover and though it had responded well to her New Year's resolution to write every day, it just wasn't the same as ink – liquid color flowing from fingertips, sensual, sensuous, wet – captured. Art taking form; expression, like paint on canvas – the work of a true artist. Handwriting, handwritten, capturing every nuance of life's history, of personality shaped and sharpened, losses, learning – all there in the ink-flow. Magical.

When she thought about what she'd just orchestrated, her smirk spread across her entire face and she could feel herself breathe as if she had a new life taking hold. She'd actually just called Jesse from the airplane phone. Jess: garbage-in, garbage-out Jess. It had been a year and a half since she'd seen him and the word "still" had finally abated. She'd recently realized it had taken as long to get to that place as she'd spent together with him. She'd been writing emails to her friends, telling them about her latest adventures, describing her garbage control theory and referring to him as, "Jesse who?"

Her friends wanted to protect her. They too wanted the "still" – always, forever – feeling to go away for her. They'd all marveled at her men stories over the years. She'd always fallen in love freely and passionately. She'd always attracted men easily. But Jesse had taken her heart like no other. Rita especially thought there was real damage attached to Jesse and what he'd done to her friend's heart. Rita didn't even want to hear Jesse's name anymore. Rita hated the pain she'd witnessed and just wanted to shake her friend so hard that all of Jesse would shatter and fly out and away, never to touch her heart again.

She and Rita had been friends since the summer after sixth grade. They'd immediately bonded when she first met Rita riding bikes in Sherwood Cemetery. She lived at the bottom of the hill, one block from the cemetery and had always loved playing there. She loved escaping to its peacefulness to lie in the grass and watch the clouds float by. She felt safe there, protected even, and never had any sense of eeriness or isolation that always spooked her other girlfriends. Her friends never wanted to go there with her and that suited her just fine.

She was riding her bike all alone, when a group of girls who didn't go to her school went biking by. One of them, a girl named Rita, stopped to talk to her and she was immediately drawn to Rita. Rita had a face full of freckles and she loved freckles, had always wanted to have them sprinkled across her nose and dusted over her cheekbones.

It was the same principle that had applied in second grade when Karen Stone had come to school wearing a clear pink eyeglasses frame. No one in their class was wearing glasses except Karen and she wanted to wear them too, just like Karen. She even exaggerated a touch on her subsequent eye examination so the doctor would prescribe them for her. And when her mother tried to get her to pick out a pretty more expensive frame, she'd insisted on the simple clear pale pink one, just like Karen's.

Much later, when she really couldn't see well enough without eyeglasses, she began to hate wearing them, yet always remembered that first pair with fondness and appreciation for Karen Stone.

Rita's freckles had kindled the same kind of envy and appreciation. Rita, of course, despised her freckles and hated the summer sun's power to bring them out. And, unlike Rita, she would never be able to acquire those much envied specks of color like Rita since her skin was richly olive and the sun only brought her even tones of golden brown.

Over the years, she and Rita had remained close although their lives had taken them down quite separate paths, far from the protected mountainsides of western Virginia where they grew up. There were lengthy periods of time when they were out of touch but in the last dozen or so years, they'd been like sisters and even closer than those early days when they'd first become such fast and dear friends.

What would Rita say if Rita knew she'd just called Jesse from the plane? Would she even tell Rita what she'd done? Rita was definitely her closest confidante. She saw Rita as her moral compass, her touchstone, her guiding light. Whether it was a fashion-forward clothes decision or a life-threatening health crisis, Rita's phone number was the one her fingers automatically reached for. Certainly, Rita had been there steadfastly through thick and thin with all of her love episodes. She felt like she was a soap opera sometimes and feared a self-indulgence that could be experienced as abusive by her loving friend.

It had begun so sweetly with Jesse:

> *When she'd first connected with Jesse, he'd stayed in her guest bedroom several nights while on a business trip to New York. He was an old acquaintance from high school and the last occurrence she'd anticipated when he came to New York was that she would fall in love with him. The final night of his time in the Apple, they'd fallen asleep on the couch in her living room after dancing to Clapton and had then slept the rest of the night curled up together in her bed.*
>
> *The next morning, they were eating breakfast at daybreak in her New York City garden and she'd asked him, "If we'd had sex last night, would you still have done spoons with me all night?" He'd replied with Southern charm, "Oh! Had you wanted to have sex with me last night?" and "Spoons! What does that mean?"*

> She'd gotten up from the table and gone inside into her kitchen and brought out two spoons to demonstrate that the way she and Jesse had slept the previous night was exactly like two spoons nestled together in the silverware drawer. After he left her that morning to drive back to Virginia, neither of them could stop thinking of the other.
>
> The following Monday, Jesse flew to New Orleans for a business trip. She took a deep breath when she opened her mailbox on Thursday to find a thick envelope from The Roosevelt Hotel in New Orleans. Inside the envelope were two perfectly nestled spoons wrapped in several of the hotel's paper cocktail napkins from the bar. She thought it was the best present she'd ever received from a man.

How could she have ever predicted such sweetness could turn so cold, could be withdrawn? She wanted to protect the safe place she'd created. She felt invincible now.

This call on the plane was the beginning of the last dance with Jesse. Even as she choreographed it with great care to make sure this time he would never feel any pressure from her to move forward into a committed future together, he still eventually gave out again; he still had to pull away; he still crushed her heart one more time.

> When she and Jesse came apart the third time and she knew she had to bury Jesse forever, she took the two spoons out to the back corner of her city garden and dug a grave for the Roosevelt Hotel spoons and placed them deep in the ground, covering them up forever with dirt and tears.

She vowed never to be in a relationship with an emotionally unavailable man again. She vowed never to be involved with a man who was in a simultaneous relationship with someone else. Over time she actually was able to live her vow never to give Jesse another chance to break her heart again.

Letting Go Messages

Joyride

She learned how important it is to:

- Keep yourself from repeating the same mistakes over and over.

- Remember you can only change yourself, not others.

- Listen to your friends; they can be objective when you can't.

- Make a commitment to recognize and protect yourself from destructive behavior.

- Gather wisdom from your life lessons so you can avoid pain and heartache in the future.

Saying Goodbye
(2002)

Death brings the ultimate letting go. When one of her most treasured friends from childhood was dying, she wrote her a letter:

Dear Marianne,

How twisted and turned around life can be. You were always the one we turned to growing up. You listened better than anyone else. You cared so deeply. You had wisdom none of us could come close to. You were the best friend anyone could have. And you abandoned us all. You simply turned your back on us and closed the door. Was it like putting an old and dear pet to sleep so he wouldn't have to face the end of his days without you? How can someone who cared so much make that kind of choice?

We had no participation in it. It was unilateral. There was nothing mutual about what you did. Now death is going to take you away from us forever this time and we are full of you once more and robbed again. What made you turn away? How is it that the best friend a person could have simply disappears and closes down to us? How do we sort out our feelings and come to terms with any of this? The past, the present and the dreaded future?

We wanted to understand and accept but it never computed. We all dealt with it on our own individual terms.

For Rita, it was as if her only sister had stabbed her in the back and left her bleeding – with her mother just buried, her job and sole means of income pulled out from under her, and the love of her life recently vanished.

For Jesse, I guess it was pure and blind acceptance. Recognizing his own history of fleeing, of closing down, of isolation, he could accept your abandonment most easily.

Your sister April, Leila, others whom you'd filled with your love – I have no sense of what they felt. I only know how wide your net was. And I became like ice toward you. I welcomed love from those in my life who were true and cut all the magnificently abundant emotional threads that tied me to you. Severed. Done. Over.

When Jesse called to tell me through Leila that you were sick, that you were dying of cancer, I listened, knowing how deeply I had loved you for so long. I searched to find the severed threads to put their ends together in some way to feel my love again. There was numbness there just like there is in my chest where my breasts used to be. There was enormous sadness in my heart for you but my feelings for you were still numb.

Rita and I talked and shared the sadness, respecting your wishes to remain disconnected. And then you reached out and asked for our contact. With each of us, it's been the same. There's been the sense of zero time lapse. We speak to you, with you, and it's as if these years between did not exist. It's as if a magician played a trick on all of us. Now you see it, now you don't – and back again. I feel taken somehow.

My love and connection were immediate as soon as we began to speak on the phone. I'm both thrilled to have those feelings back and resentful too. I'll now have to lose you and let go all over again. And I'll have to put this all together somehow and live with it in its new form. I'm laughing, thinking of our conversation this morning, of your need to organize and alphabetize everything. So where do I put all of this? How do I put all of this in order?

I turn to my strongest beliefs, convictions really – my knowing, in every fiber of my being, the beauty of loss. Nothing can bring about deeper appreciation than losing what you treasure most. Life would be hollow and pitiful without loss. Life would actually have no beauty at all without loss. These recent times have magnified this awareness one hundred-fold. The World Trade Center, my father's death, Jesse gone for the third time – and now you, my dearest Marianne.

And so I begin with mostly questions. And so I begin with a letter to you, pronouncing my belief in the beauty of loss. And so I begin with a vow to use my word-blessed gift of expression. I vow to write about and unravel pain, to search for meaning in chaos and loss, and to seek ways to soothe all of our aching hearts.

She never sent the letter to Marianne. Writing it filled her with both sadness and satisfaction. She didn't attend Marianne's funeral; she couldn't deal; the conflicting feelings still persisted. She carried too much pain and emptiness from how Marianne had never given any explanation nor spoken about the reason for the disappearance and disconnection for all those years. She would never know what turned Marianne away, what made Marianne shut down.

Rita traveled from New England to Virginia to be there at Marianne's graveside to say her last goodbye. She saw how Rita was able to put it all behind much more quickly than she could. Whenever she thought of Marianne she would breathe in and feel a haunting emptiness in her chest pushing against her ribs.

She promised herself she would place her faith and emotion in those who were true.

Letting Go Messages

Saying Goodbye

She learned how important it is to:

- Use your losses to build appreciation for what remains.

- Realize that permanence is an illusion, and all you have will be replaced by the new now.

- Appreciate how love can endure in your historic heart even when betrayal has captured its possibility in your present world.

- Treasure and honor your true, true friends.

- Find a way to accept that you may never know the cause of friendship's end.

Matthew

B.B. King's
(2002)

She was recuperating from Jesse. She knew she could never go back there again. Three times he'd suddenly left her. There was no warning it was coming. They'd never argued. They'd never been without passion and connection. He just suddenly HAD to leave. He said he experienced love as pressure. She would call it "Turtle Time" – the time when he claimed he had no choice except to withdraw, pull his head and heart inside his shell, disappear.

Once he'd even explained how overwhelming the compulsion to flee had always been, ending his description with, "I know I've hurt a lot of people in my life but I'm okay with that."

This third time was going to be the last time. She hadn't been with Jesse for almost six months, since the end of September right after the planes had flown into the World Trade towers, since the end of September when her father had died.

She had such resolve. She felt cleansed somehow. She would never again be with a man who was in another simultaneous relationship. She would never be with someone with intimacy issues. She would never be with someone who wasn't really available. Enough! Uncle! Basta! Assez!

After a long winter's healing, she started to date again. She decided to go to B.B. King's to hear Delbert McClinton. Jesse had introduced her to Delbert's music. She and Jesse had shared and "owned" Delbert and Clapton and Boz Scaggs – their music, their songs, their singers. Jesse had introduced her to Scaggs too but Clapton belonged to her. She'd danced with Jesse to *Pilgrim*, her new Clapton album, in her living room, the night she'd fallen in love with Jesse. Clapton's wrap-around, beckoning voice; his lamenting, steamy, guitar riffs; and the neither slow nor fast rhythm of "My Father's Eyes" had pulled her feet in perfect sync with Jesse's. Her heart was captured, in his possession, as they moved together barefoot, gliding, if not floating, across the pickled, beach-like, parquet floor.

Four years later, the night she met Matthew at B.B. King's, she had a date with a giant (6'10"). The Giant was ... well, a giant, really a giant; he was also an avid and constant Bridge player; he ate, drank and breathed Bridge. It just hadn't seemed like a great match. She'd given Bridge a try a few times but it wasn't her game. She was more of a Scrabble or Backgammon kind of woman. They did share some music interests. He'd been excited about going to a Delbert concert. McClinton was sold out that night and The Giant had a back problem so she'd agreed to go ahead of time and stand in line for Standing Room Only tickets or, better still perhaps, tickets from someone who'd bought extra seats or was unable to use two already purchased tickets. Since there were no assigned seats for tickets at B.B. King's, she was going early and felt sure she would be able to snag two tickets.

When she got there, there were two men already waiting in line for SRO tickets. The three of them fell into a typical waiting-in-line kind of conversation. The man who was first in line was a downer guy full of pessimism, "We'll never get in; Delbert's been sold out for weeks."

She and the second guy naturally progressed to another line of dialogue about how much they loved Delbert and how they were confident they'd get in since they were so close to the front of the line. His name was Matthew and he lived in San Francisco.

"Of course we'll get in." Matthew said. "It's a couple of hours before show time and we're at the front of the line for Standing Room tickets. Maybe we'll even be lucky enough to get seated down front."

At some point, a person came along with an extra ticket and the pessimist got his chance to go in and be seated; for sure he would end up close to the stage; it was still early. Matthew and she continued to talk. He was very chatty and pleasant and they clicked easily talking about music. He worked for a social services counseling agency in San Francisco specializing in teen delinquency and was a consultant in the field of not-for-profit fundraising. He had a very ruddy complexion and seemed to be blushing most of the time. He was lanky with a thin neck, narrow shoulders, and long lean fingers; she didn't see his wedding band but did notice his thick curly reddish blond hair, sprinkled with white; bizarrely, most likely he was wearing a toupee. He was around her height, maybe a touch taller and just seemed like a good ol' nice guy. She'd always liked tall men but had actually been very uncomfortable recently being anywhere in public with The Giant. Several times she'd commented, "It's like dating an announcement!"

She'd always been very outgoing and friendly yet had also always coveted her privacy. Walking down the street with The Giant had felt like a thief had stolen her prized anonymity, one of the elements she'd always loved about living in New York City. Somehow The Giant had served a great purpose to make her more appreciative and comfortable with a short man like Matthew.

Not too long after the first pessimist guy had gotten his ticket to get in to see Delbert, someone else showed up with two tickets to sell. Since Matthew, who was next in line, only needed one ticket, he stepped aside to let her buy these tickets for The Giant and her. The person selling the tickets was very concerned about getting caught as a scalper even though the asking-price was the face value of the tickets. The seller insisted on going way down the block on 42nd Street to complete the transaction. On her way back to B.B. King's after purchasing her tickets, she stopped to say thank you again to Matthew, who was still in line hoping to get a seated ticket, and gave him her business card.

She then left the second ticket for The Giant at the Will-Call window and went inside. She knew B.B. King's was a first come/first seated venue and she wanted to be up front as close to Delbert as possible. She would try to save a seat for The Giant but she really wasn't going to worry about where he would end up sitting if it turned out she was unable to save a place for him.

Well over an hour later, when the room was packed, when almost every seat was filled, when the bar area in the back was crammed with Standing Room Only audience members, and when food had been ordered and eaten, for some odd reason, diagonally across from where she was sitting at a table actually abutting the stage, there was one empty seat. The Giant still hadn't arrived, when a barmaid with a big tip in her pocket brought Matthew from his SRO place at the bar all the way down front to that empty seat across from her. It kind of took her breath away to see him suddenly sitting right there in front of her. There were probably eight hundred people there, with 650 of them seated. Her table was next to the stage where seats were of the highest premium and had, of course, filled very early. How had he ended up right where she was sitting? How had that one seat stayed empty? "Hello, Matthew. What a nice surprise!"

Matthew had never gotten a ticket for a seat and had ended up inside to stand at the bar area in the very back of the room. He'd asked a server to try to find him an empty seat somewhere and this was the only one that could be located. He proceeded to introduce himself to the people at the table as the proud husband of a wife who would soon be earning a Ph.D. degree and as an avid runner who'd run every day for fourteen years.

As everyone listened to Delbert's great opening act and then to Delbert, she became completely absorbed in and deeply touched by the music and frequently had tears spilling from her eyes. The Giant had finally arrived and had found another empty seat exactly behind where she was sitting at the next table over. She was pretty sure those two empty seats had most likely been the only two remaining seats in the entire place.

When everyone was fighting the masses at the end of the evening to leave B.B. King's and The Giant had gone to the coat-check line to get their coats, she and Matthew chatted some more.

"I was very touched by your tears while you were listening to the music tonight."

"Yeah, well, I'm healing from a broken heart and Delbert and his music really connect me back to the guy who broke it."

She sensed how genuine and sensitive he seemed to be. She liked his openness and appreciated how observant he was. The Giant had noticed nothing about her experience of the music or certainly not indicated if he had. There'd been plenty of tears running down her cheeks as she'd gotten lost in Delbert's songs.

Matthew mentioned where he was staying a half block from Central Park West and how much he loved that location because of how convenient it was for running. "I love running in Central Park," she said and asked him if he wanted to run there together in the morning.

He blew her off, "Oh I'm sure you don't want to get up that early. I'm planning on running before 6:00 AM so I can make it to JFK by 8:30 to catch my flight back to San Francisco."

They all said good bye outside the entrance to B. B. King's. She and The Giant headed west on 42nd Street to go to Chez Josephine for a late supper and Matthew headed to the subway to take the #1 train up to Columbus Circle.

Letting Go Messages

B.B. King's

She learned how important it is to:

- Be aware how new horizons are always just beyond what you can see from where you are now.

- Gain from loss and know it adds to the richness of your capacity to live a fuller life.

- Recognize how people may have motives different from the ones they declare.

- Live and love with a full heart, extending the trust you want to receive in return.

- Keep your receptivity vibrant and alive even when you've gained ample wounds and scars that contribute to resistance and suspicion.

Living Blind
(2002)

She was taken by total surprise to find an email from Matthew in her inbox on Tuesday following the Friday night she'd met him at B.B. King's. She'd completely forgotten she'd given him her business card. In his email, he told her it was his birthday and commented about how much he loved candles and music and such. He was consoling about her painful breakup with the boyfriend she'd told him about at B.B. King's. He mentioned his wife's graduate studies. It felt like he was presenting himself as a wonderful non-romantic new friend.

When she replied to his email, she told him everyone called her The Candle Lady because of the vast number of candles always burning everywhere in her home and City garden. She mentioned her birthday was the following month on the same day of the month as his. She wrote about music.

She asked him if he could introduce her to Mister Right. He replied back, "I know a Doctor *Wright* who is married so that would make him Doctor *Wrong*."

The correspondence seemed very innocent and platonic and she appreciated it since her heart was aching so much from the loss of Jesse and since she was disinterested in a romantic involvement. During a previous "time-out" from Jesse, she'd met a lovely married man who was a retired judge from Australia. They'd sat in adjacent seats on an airplane flight and had started an email correspondence afterwards. When the judge subsequently traveled to New York they'd gone to theater and museums and restaurants together and it had been so pleasant to have a male friend to be with who was married and wasn't going to put any unwanted moves on her. She'd welcomed that friendship and saw Matthew as exactly that kind of guy.

Matthew and she emailed back and forth over the next few weeks and on her birthday she received a box addressed to The Candle Lady. It contained a beautiful big fat candle with hydrangea flowers carved in the wax and a CD with a wonderful music compilation Matthew had made just for her. She particularly loved two songs on it by singer songwriters she didn't know. One was Lucy Kaplansky and the other was Chuck Brodsky.

It turned out Matthew was coming back to New York for a conference at the end of April. He asked her if she'd like to go with him to a Chuck Brodsky house concert in New Jersey while Matthew was in town. She wrote she'd love to and told him she had a car and could drive them there.

It was a special day; they had the time in the car for long conversations; the house concert was delightful; she really liked Chuck. When they got back to the City, they decided to go to her favorite place, Gramercy Tavern, to have dinner in the informal tavern at the front of the restaurant.

After they were seated and had ordered two glasses of New Zealand Malbec and cassoulet with fennel, Matthew began to pour out his heart to her. He described a first marriage that lasted two minutes; he called it his starter marriage. He told her of Denise, the crazy mother of his two daughters, whom he'd never married, and how he'd gotten custody of and raised the girls. With a pained expression on his face, he told her about his second wife Lola, "She adored my two daughters and they adored her. Lola also adored my best friend Dan and had an affair with him."

When she saw him wipe away the tears ready to fall from his eyes as he talked about Lola and Dan's betrayal leading to an extremely painful divorce, her heart went out to him and how hurtful it must have been. She silently reflected, "I can't even begin to imagine what it would feel like to have a spouse cheat on you with your best friend."

She thought she'd heard him say Dan was still his best friend twenty years later, but that just couldn't be true. How could he still be best friends with someone who'd had an affair with his wife? No, she must have misunderstood…

She was surprised when he told her about his "dead" marriage of fifteen years to his current third wife, Tina. He said Tina had lost interest in intimacy and they hadn't been together sexually in over five years. "I've always been faithful to her and have never slept with any other women."

Tina had been working on her PhD for eight years and would be graduating and getting her degree in June. "I intend to tell Tina I want a divorce as soon as she's completed her doctoral program. I really care about her but I'm not in love with her anymore.

"We've really grown apart since Tina started graduate school and I definitely want to have intimacy in my life again. Tina went through a horrible divorce from her first husband and I know how upsetting a second divorce is going to be for her. To tell you the truth, I think no matter how bad things have gotten between us, she's determined never to be divorced again. This is going to be so hard for her. I want to wait until Tina's got that diploma in her hands before I tell her I want a divorce."

She hadn't expected to learn he was living in a failed marriage because from the moment he'd introduced himself to everyone at B.B. King's the night she'd first met him, he'd spoken often and with so much pride about how smart Tina was and about her becoming Doctor Tina Scudder. His tenderness was touching and set him apart from most of the men she'd known.

At the end of the meal at Gramercy Tavern, she and Matthew walked out onto Twentieth Street as the last light of the sunset was fading into a blood orange ribbon to the west in New Jersey. They agreed to meet for a light dinner around seven o'clock three nights later, to say goodbye before Matthew flew back to San Francisco.

When that night arrived, she didn't feel well. She was lightheaded and slightly dizzy and needed to lie down. She left Matthew a message letting him know she wasn't feeling well enough to meet him but if he wanted to stop by, she would leave the door unlocked to her apartment and he could let himself in and come upstairs to talk quietly in the dark with her for a little while.

Matthew was very respectful and attentive and sat in the rocking chair across from her bed and read poems to her he said he'd written about her the night he met her at B.B King's. One of them was called "The New York Fool," referring to Jesse whose name he hadn't known nor had he known Jesse lived in Virginia. She was enthralled with the poetry and told Matthew, "These poems are better than spoons!"

It was as if the words Matthew had written were a salve that could dissolve the pain she'd been feeling from losing Jesse. Those spoons had existed as a symbol of irreplaceable love even though she'd buried them in the ground to deny their existence. Matthew's poems were gifts, woven from words, created anew just for her. The healing she felt and the connection that emerged from these poems filled and soothed her. She felt her heartache melting away for the first time since her last goodbye with Jesse.

She shared how Jesse had sent her two nestled spoons and explained to Matthew their symbolic meaning. "I buried those spoons in my New York City garden to make sure I'd never let Jessie back into my heart."

Matthew appreciated her story of the spoons and was pleased he'd outshone Jesse with his poetry gifts that had such high value, such special priceless significance to her. "It means the world to me my poems could take away some of your pain."

As she and Matthew corresponded, spent time together in New York, spoke on the phone and became closer, she learned about Matthew's difficult childhood. He had a very hard time talking about the ridicule he'd grown up with. His pale skin, slender delicate body and constantly flushed face had made him the butt of many cruel jokes.

She felt such connected sweet sympathy for him when he described the time a group of sixth grade boys had barricaded him in one of the stalls in the Boys' bathroom and taken his pants from him. He'd been too embarrassed to cry out for someone to help him or crawl out from the stall pants-less.

That afternoon he was supposed to be giving his big presentation on Denmark, his father's homeland, in Geography class. He'd proudly brought to school that

Living Blind

morning a big red oak-tag poster board where he'd carefully placed two pieces of wide white opaque tape to replicate the horizontal band and vertical band that configure the white cross on the red Danish flag. He'd stenciled bold black letters representing Denmark's geography across the horizontal white bar of the cross: "The Jutland Peninsula: Land of Islands."

In 1956, Oak Lane Elementary School in Oakland, California was massively overcrowded with kids from housing projects, many of whom couldn't speak English. The teachers were severely overworked and the class sizes were so enormous that the Geography teacher who happened to be a substitute teacher never noticed Matthew's absence even though he was scheduled to make his report that day.

He'd stared at the cracked and moldy tiles behind the toilet, watching the toil of a spider and waiting until after the end of the school day to crawl out from the stall. He'd found and wrapped himself in a sawdust-laden carpenter's apron from the mechanic's shop to cover his faded-to-gray tighty-whities, unsuccessfully trying to hide the huge frayed hole exposing his left butt cheek.

Matthew had walked all the way home as the sky began to darken, with the cumbersome buckskin apron dragging the sidewalk, to avoid the stares and jeers he'd have had to endure if he'd taken the bus. His bus pass was in the pants they took away from him anyway.

Matthew was in the middle of a bizarre growth surge where his legs seemed to be spurting out beneath him every day, like Pinocchio's nose that grew longer whenever he told a lie. He'd been feeling like it must have been his fault his father had died so suddenly and that he was being punished for it, that his legs were growing to generate more of Matthew to fill the gaping emptiness of no longer having a father.

He possessed only two pairs of pants that fit him and was really hoping to find the pair taken from him by the gang of boys. His mother's wrath for the missing pants would add too much insult to the damaging injuries he'd already suffered that day. His mother had been working such long hours since his father died and money for another pair of new pants would be hard to come by. He was glad she wouldn't get back from work until after eight o'clock and wasn't going to see him arrive home disheveled without his pants.

Matthew and his mother lived in the Tassafaronga public housing development, built to provide cheap housing for workers at the shipyards along the Oakland Inner Harbor Channel. His father had been a welder and Matthew went to bed every night after his father died, fretting he and his mother were going to be kicked out of their home.

The next morning, he pulled the covers over his head and begged his mother to let him stay home from school. "We'll have none of that this morning, Laddy Boy." She basically dragged him from the bed and soon shoved him out the door without breakfast which he always refused to eat anyway. The cardboard-tasting porridge she made every morning made him gag. She'd become frail and depleted in the last few months. Matthew suspected his mother had stopped eating altogether. Lately she always had a can of beer by her side which she sipped slowly, always keeping the can concealed inside a small brown paper bag. He worried about his mother's drinking but the constant scent of the beer on her breath and from her sweat reminded him of his father and gave him comfort.

His mother had never even asked him how his Denmark report had gone the previous day. She'd completed inking in most of the lettering on his poster when his little fingers had become cramped from bearing down so hard on the markers and because he kept smearing the black ink when he lifted the stencil to start a new letter.

When he got to the bottom of the stairwell that opened onto the lobby of the building where they lived, he noticed something odd behind the bottom step. There were no risers on the stairs and as he peered through the open space between the last two steps, he simultaneously saw and smelled his urine-saturated pants. The stench was so strong that he figured every one of those boys had to have peed on his purloined pants. Wrapped around the filthy trousers, cinching them into a sort of tube-like formation, was the white tape from his long-labored Denmark poster. The letters had been transformed into smudges blurred so badly they were indistinguishable.

Matthew's anger became much bigger than his sadness as his eyes burned and watered from the urine fumes. He used a thick gnarled branch that had fallen from the one old tree in front of the building to push the pants out through the doorway, across the dusty courtyard, down off the curb and into the gutter drain.

While running away as fast as he could, his book-bag banging against his legs, to get as far as possible from the shameful ruined evidence, he said a prayer aloud to the heavens, "Blessed Mary, Mother of God, Sweet Angel of Mercy, I beg of you, keep my mother's eyes far from those pants. Oh please don't let her see them there in the gutter on her way to work. Protect me and keep me safe. In your dear son Jesus' name I pray. Amen!"

At lunch, he stared out of the dingy low windows with the chicken wire embedded in the glass along the back wall of the cafeteria. In his mind, he was constructing the story he would swear as truth if confronted by his mother about his missing pants. As his eyes scanned the layers of debris behind the school, he glimpsed the bent and mangled corner of his red oak-tag poster sticking out from the top of the trash-filled dumpster down below.

"My mother never did find out about my missing pants," Matthew declared to her. "Warren Stanley, the cousin of the ringleader of the boys who'd ganged up on me, approached me at recess that next day and quickly handed me a Western Department Store bag with a slightly used pair of khaki pants inside that were a couple shades darker and one size bigger than the ones that had been taken. The coolest part of all was these pants had what everyone called back then a 'hiney-binder' which was a four-inches long, buckled strap that went right across the small of the back just below the waistband."

"Oh, I remember those." she laughed, "If you didn't have a hiney-binder on the back of your pants, you just weren't cool, right?"

"Well, I'd never had a pair of pants with that coveted hiney-binder and felt like it had all been worth it when I looked down inside that bag and saw my new treasure. Warren had looked back over each of his shoulders and said, 'Don't say anything to my cousin Ed or anybody else about this, okay?' and then he just walked away as if he'd never spoken to me.

"I don't know which was the worst part of the story," Matthew added at the end of recounting his boyhood saga, "that they'd taken my pants or that they could hear me sobbing in the bathroom like a little baby. Ever since that day, I've shed tears at the drop of a pin. My daughters tell everyone their father is so emotional that he cries at the opening of shopping centers.

"I never went in the Boys' bathroom again for the next two years. I would somehow find a way to wander off during recess or lunch and pee, hidden between the huge dumpster and the giant oak tree at the back of the school.

"I feel like I can tell you anything. ... like I can tell you everything." he comfortably confided to her.

She was definitely an attentive and reinforcing listener. She saw how, when Matthew tried to tell her about his most painful memories, the tears would start to collect in his eyes and often he wouldn't be able to keep talking because some odd form of uncontrollable guffaws of laughter would take over. It was strange to see him laughing almost panic-stricken, his eyes brimming with tears, and with extreme and desperate sadness in his facial expression. She could sense how badly he'd been wounded growing up.

She never said anything to Matthew about the insurmountable damage she saw linking the humiliating Boys' bathroom assault to the sudden death of Matthew's father at age forty-seven, just four months prior. On the day of his father's funeral, Matthew's father's sister, his Aunt Alma, had picked him up and pushed his face into his father's coffin forcing him to kiss his dead father goodbye. Matthew had nightmares about his father's funeral for years. He'd probably never kissed his father when he was alive. His father had been a good deal older than his mother, an austere and cold man who rarely spoke to anyone and almost never acknowledged Matthew's presence altogether. Matthew could not remember ever seeing his father touch his mother.

She realized Matthew was falling in love with her. She didn't want to be romantically involved with a married man. She told Matthew he would have to be separated from his wife if he wanted to move forward with her. She made no commitments to him and even told him plainly, "I'm giving you no promise of any kind to be there for you if you get divorced." She told him she never wanted to have a romantic or physical relationship with a married man.

She did insist on two promises from Matthew though. She asked him to swear he would not use her as a reason to leave his wife; he had to promise her he would not leave Tina for her.

She also told him how she felt about honesty. She told him she'd made a vow to refrain from telling any falsehoods to anyone; she'd promised herself to tell the truth always. She told him she required a promise he would not lie to his wife about anything, that he would never lie to anyone. He swore these two oaths to her quickly the moment she requested them.

Matthew told her again how he wanted to wait until Tina had graduated and earned her PhD to say he wanted a divorce. She appreciated how caring and protective Matthew was of his wife's feelings. She accepted his need to postpone this conversation.

"I understand the reasons for your putting off telling Tina you want a divorce until her graduation but I don't want to hear from you or have any contact at all with you again until you've told her you want a divorce and are separated."

Right after the graduation weekend, after the visiting friends left who'd been celebrating Tina's years of hard work and achievement, Matthew called to tell her he'd told Tina he wanted a divorce. She felt sad for Tina but was ecstatic to hear Matthew's voice again and to know she could move forward with him in a more open and intimate way. Even though the separation of silence had lasted for less than a month, she'd felt deprived of Matthew's contact and had achingly missed him.

"I did it!" he proclaimed.

When she heard his voice on the phone telling her he'd asked Tina for a divorce, she almost couldn't hear his words because her heart was pounding so loudly.

Letting Go Messages

Living Blind

She learned how important it is to:

- Realize and value when rare and priceless gifts come your way.

- Venture beyond what you already know and stretch your mind until your final day.

- Seek out and identify the deeper meaning and motivation beneath the surface.

- Find tangible ways and rituals to cut damaging ties and finalize what needs to be in the past.

- Take time to get to know someone well before moving a relationship to a deeper level.

SANCTUARY
(2003)

For every person there's only one true sanctuary; it lies within and there's no external entity, personal relationship, or material possession that can fill the void of a lost and searching soul. People who look to religious faith, wealth, and social status to gain a sense of worth still come up feeling empty. True well-being is derived from inside oneself. She learned this again and again, most often through facing life daringly, taking grand risks, overcoming hardship and coping with loss.

She remembered her early days as a divorced woman, when she felt disenfranchised without the identity and protection of her wealthy husband, Hank, The Banker. Going alone to a social event, a movie or a restaurant was sickeningly painful back then.

For years she wanted to have a house in the country. She bought antique furniture – an oak deacon's bench, a charming pine desk – for the country house she would have one day. Her friend Nan stored the desk and bench for her in a barn on a farm outside of Rhinebeck.

She talked about her country-home desire frequently and always coupled it with the concept that first she needed to find a man so she could make this vision a reality. It was as if she truly believed there was an actual requirement for her to be married, that the man would be the necessary first hurdle for her to be allowed to have a house in the country (that, of course, the man would buy for her).

Time passed. She gained her place in the world as a single woman. She went to movies, restaurants and events alone and felt solid and strong in her own skin with her own identity. She built her professional life and thrived as an author, coach and consultant. She nourished old and new friendships. She fell in love, she had her heart broken more than once, she healed and grew into a fuller person. She became a solid skier, an avid fisherwoman, a fierce tennis competitor and an outdoor enthusiast. Music filled her life. She lost her sister to breast cancer, she had prophylactic bilateral mastectomy surgery, she bought a dog. The World Trade Towers fell. Her father died. Time passed.

The house-in-the-country dream lived on and always felt like something somehow someday ... in the future.

There was a confluence of events that brought about the right mix of ingredients to make her wish come true:

> *1. For sure, the impact of 9/11 was huge, bringing an overwhelming appreciation of being a survivor – of simply having air to breathe and life to live. Along with that appreciation came a driving awareness of how finite and precious time is. Unquestionably, the impact of 9/11 was the biggest factor in her making a decision to take the big leap to find and buy a house in the country.*

> *2. One afternoon she ran into her feisty neighbor Alice as she rounded the corner on Park Avenue. Alice was a psychologist who lived in the building across the street from her. Alice was out walking her adorable wirehaired dachshund, Max. She and Alice often stopped to chat and share their wild enthusiasm for dogs. As Alice talked about driving Upstate that afternoon, she and Alice quickly fell into a conversation about buying a house in the country. She learned Alice had owned her house in Tivoli for seventeen years and there was no man in Alice's life then nor when the house was bought. Alice berated her quite a bit. "What makes you think you need a man to purchase a house in the country?! What makes you think you need a man to do anything you want to do? How old are you, darlin'? When exactly do you think you're going to have this dream of yours come true?!" She walked away from Alice with her bubble burst and her eyes wide open.*

> 3. Shortly after the in-your-face conversation with Alice, she went to theater one night with her dear friends, Harold and Ron. They were very excited because they'd just bought an old Victorian house in the country in a small village on the west side of the Hudson River she knew well from having fished off the lighthouse there many summers before. It was quite inspiring to listen to Harold and Ron describe the house and share how much they paid for it. The seed was definitely planted and sprouting. She could do this. She would do this. She was 56 years old. If not then, when?

Real life always had so much more irony in it than the fiction she ardently and appreciatively read about in novels. She'd finally decided to buy a house in the country completely on her own without the help or participation of a man and right there planted squarely in her life, claiming total devotion to her, was Matthew; steady, adoring, dedicated Matthew. He lived far away just outside of San Francisco. He was not going to be her husband. Matthew was great with technology but was not good with tools or fixing things like her father, her former husband and her old love Jesse. Matthew barely had "a pot to piss in" and she knew she couldn't count on him for financial or handyman support of any kind.

As a result of Matthew's getting a divorce from Tina, he was going to have to give up the house he'd lived in for over eighteen years. His girls had grown up in that house but they were both married and had lives and homes of their own. Tina had made most of the mortgage payments over the years so he had no choice as the divorce moved forward other than to put the house on the market.

Matthew would certainly be thrilled and supportive of her quest and happy to share her joy and take pleasure in country life with her but he would be unable to contribute tangibly or provide dollars toward the purchase or upkeep of her house. It would be all hers.

She looked at many houses. A friend of Harold and Ron's found a house online on the other side of the river which she almost bought. Her friend Nan was a real estate agent and made it a goal to find the right house for her. Nan showed her many houses in a wide range of communities on both sides of the Hudson. None of them felt right.

The moment she climbed over the deep snow bank and stepped onto the dilapidated front porch of the old 1830s farmhouse at the top of the hill less than a mile from Harold and Ron's newly purchased house, she felt a deep connection stirring inside her. She'd told Nan she didn't want to renovate a house. She'd wanted to find a house that was walk-in ready for her, a house that needed nothing done to it. The farmhouse was a wreck.

Many of the rooms were piled with junk although it was completely unfurnished; no one had lived there since the summer. Among many unwanted objects scattered everywhere, there was a dead plant on the kitchen counter and a box of half used diapers nearby on the floor. In the living room there was some kind of animal skin rug laid down all cockeyed in ripples and a pile of clothes on wire hangers strewn across the floor along with a wood-burning stove in the middle of the hearth in front of the gorgeous stone fireplace.

Next to the fireplace sitting on one of the shelves of a primitive makeshift built-in bookcase there was an air conditioner with a big thick electric cord tumbling down exposed in front of the book shelves with the back of the air conditioner jutting out on the other side of the living room wall behind the bookcase into the enclosed sun porch that wrapped around the side of the house. In addition to the ugly back of the air conditioning unit sticking out obtrusively, the cinderblock back of the fireplace was hideously exposed. The long narrow graceful floor space of the sun porch was covered in tools, debris and a couple of utilitarian work tables.

As she walked through the house with all of its clutter and saw all it needed and all she wanted to do to it, she kept repeating aloud over and over, "I hate you, Nan. I hate you, Nan. I hate you Nan. I hate you, Nan."

She was totally captivated by this house and saw its charm in spite of all its covered-up beauty and screaming needs. It had the magnificent river stone fireplace. It had views of the Berkshire Mountains. It had a big wide covered front porch. It had the long completely windowed sun porch. It had a great deck in the back off the kitchen. It had a big old weathered ready-to-fall-down barn. It had a workroom in the basement that immediately connected her to her father who always had a workroom in the basement wherever they lived and who had just recently passed away. It had old charm and didn't look like any of the other houses she'd seen. She wanted it!

Because of the heavy snow that winter, she never saw the roof of the house until well after she'd put a deposit on it and started the lengthy inspection, contract negotiation and getting-the-owner-to-empty the house and barn process. One day just before the closing, she drove up to check things out and found all three of the owner's daughters, ages four to thirteen, carrying stuff up the hill from the barn to a truck parked in the driveway with their father sitting on the front porch steps doing nothing but watching them. The closing took place on July 2nd, her former husband Hank's 58th birthday, a nice little twist to not needing a man to purchase a house. The entire family who'd lived in the house was present and when the wife handed her a second set of keys to the house as they were leaving the law offices where the closing took place, the youngest little girl, who was being carried out wrapped in her mother's arms, burst into tears of deep and pure sadness for the goodbye to the farmhouse where this child had lived and played since her birth.

With zero experience in home ownership and a gaping lack of knowledge about house renovation, she took on this quest fearlessly and boldly. She became her own General Contractor for the project and the men she hired to do the work respected her courage and became her friends. The carpenter, plumber, electrician and painter all lived on the same road the house was on within five miles in either direction. She treated them all with great respect and not one of them ever took advantage of her lack of knowledge and experience or her gender.

There was complete electrical and heating system updating required. She added two full bathrooms to the house, one upstairs and one down; she removed and added walls; she added and replaced windows, bringing magnificent light and cross-ventilated air into the stuffy darkness and opening up soothing vistas of the Berkshires that had been obscured and had cried for viewing. She replaced the ugly heavy slider door from the dining room to the sun porch with French doors and tore down the bookshelf in the living room replacing the entire wall next to the fireplace with another set of French doors opening onto the sun porch, creating light and openness in the living room and providing graciousness and elegance to a space that had been dark, ordinary and lackluster in its former iteration.

She created and installed a completely reconfigured kitchen, turning the kitchen, dining room and sun porch into a Great Room inviting social flow and entertainment for guests, for parties and for her own enjoyment. The flow emanated from the welcoming new kitchen where she would provide nourishment for herself and others.

From Labor Day to Halloween, the demo and renovation work inside the house took place. She was patient with the workers yet very impatient for the work to be completed. She regularly made the two-hour trip each way to inspect the progress often stopping at Lowe's in Kingston on her way up or on her way back to the City, to select and purchase windows, faucets, light fixtures, plumbing supplies, kitchen cabinets, appliances, wainscoting, stairway spindles and on and on.

On October 26th, her grandmother's birthday, she, her mother, and her little dog arrived along with the 20' Penske truck driven by her dear childhood friend Gail's son Gus. Gus had learned to drive a big truck as part of his missionary work in South America. In the Star City, Gus picked up furniture of her mother's and grandmother's that had been in storage, as well as new furniture and rugs from three retail locations, and a beautiful antique red wardrobe for her master bedroom, purchased from Julie, another beloved friend from childhood. On the way north, Gus stopped in Maryland to pick up her mother's and father's first dining room furniture that had been at her niece's home in Deale, Maryland, and then on to one more stop in New York City for all of the dishes, pots and pans, and coveted items she'd been buying, collecting and storing in her city closets to have one day for that house in the country. She'd recently gotten her bench and desk from Nan's Rhinebeck farm so Gus didn't have to make another stop on his long trek from Virginia to the Hudson Valley.

It was happening. She and her mother slept in one bed together that first night in the country house she'd bought without the participation, help or support of a husband. It had taken only seven weeks to complete such a huge amount of renovation work. It had felt like it took seven years.

There was still the front porch to be rebuilt and the outside of the house needed painting. These would be done in the spring. The crowning culmination to her renovation project would be the garage gazebo, stone walls and gardens that would be completed at the end of the summer and early fall.

As the house came to life through the renovations, furnishings, artwork and objects she brought to it, she and Matthew christened the house "The Sanctuary." It became a haven and escape where all felt harm-free and protected. Being there was like going back in time. It reminded her of her Star City childhood in the mountains of western Virginia. The sheltering mountains and simpler life encircled her and she felt safe there.

She made wonderful friends. She kayaked and fished. She hiked and skied. She toured the beautiful historic homes along the Hudson. She went antiquing. She immersed herself in the Hudson Valley music scene, gathering singer-songwriters around her whom she worshipped and adored. Matthew discovered The John Street Jam in Saugerties where the best music was performed every month and where she found wonderful friendships she would always cherish. She threw two fabulous Solstice music parties in The Sanctuary every year which she called "Sing for Your Supper Solstice Celebration." She prepared delicious feasts for these parties, saying she was on kitchen duty since she didn't play a musical instrument and couldn't sing. It saddened her beyond expression her voice couldn't match the perfect pitch she heard inside her ears. She shared literature and the spoken word at these Solstice parties, reading aloud selected lyrical passages from the novels she loved.

There were two local couples that grew to be like family. There was Maggie and Gary. Maggie was a combination of Martha Stewart and Mother Earth. Her home was immaculate and her cooking was spectacular. Every holiday brought seasonal decoration inside and out. Gary was the handyman's handyman. He could fix anything and if he wasn't physically moving or repairing something, he wasn't happy. There was Paul and Carina. Everyone in the community knew them and depended on them for help. Paul was the good Samaritan that came to people's rescue in projects big or small. Carina was easy-going and faithful. She always had a smile on her face and shied away from politics and serious conversation.

Along with Matthew, they became a gang of six and she spent almost as much time in their houses as she did in her own whenever she came Upstate from the City. They all loved to cook and socialize at home. They played dominos, backgammon and Scrabble.

They laughed and had great fun together. They celebrated life.

She felt surrounded and protected by love.

Letting Go Messages

Sanctuary

She learned how important it is to:

- Eliminate dependency from your life.

- Do all you can to be the one who makes your dreams come true.

- Erase the blocks keeping you from getting what's important to you.

- Recognize most barriers exist only in your head.

- Leverage inspiration to risk doing what you've never done.

Balancing Act
(2013)

She knew the value of her evolution, experiencing and trusting its unyielding weight. Alongside this clear knowledge was her awareness of the threatening potential of her tendency to sweep away that kind of weight as if it were a feather in a storm. She knew she was on new ground and wholeheartedly trusted her feelings and convictions. She was paying her penance for past damage with an open and abundantly willing heart.

For over ten years she'd taken Matthew's adoring love for granted with a good deal of condescension about what she considered to be major blocks, missing links and less than good-enough-for-her characteristics, like a Goddess of Entitlement for whom no man could measure up. She could see how she'd interpreted insignificant and unimportant traits and behaviors of Matthew's into character flaws.

There was the photo taken on the front porch at Cedar Grove, The Thomas Cole House in Catskill, on Black Friday, the first Thanksgiving weekend they spent Upstate in 2003, soon after she bought the house in the country. As Gary announced the traditional "Say Cheese!" to take their photo, she felt Matthew, beside her, lift himself onto his toes to gain a few inches of height. She'd looked at photos with Matthew in them and wondered how he always seemed taller in the photos than she thought his actual height was. Her judgment against his tippy-toe stance was rather harsh and when they had some privacy later and she got the nerve to confront him, he feigned complete ignorance. "I have no awareness of doing that!" he claimed. "It doesn't make sense or have a purpose. Why would I?" He protested vehemently, displaying hurt pride for being inaccurately portrayed and falsely accused.

When they picked up her car from the dealership that afternoon, Matthew chose to wait outside in the brisk November air rather than sit in the toasty warm showroom. When she drove around the building to pick him up, after he patiently waited for her to finish the paperwork, he slipped into the passenger seat, explaining his new discovery, "I was out there in the cold, rubbing my hands together to make up for leaving my gloves in Gary's car, when I saw that I was rocking back on my heels and then up on my toes to get warm. I never realized I did anything like that. Obviously, this is some kind of unconscious habit I have when I get cold. Now it makes complete sense why I rolled up on my toes at Cedar Grove." He'd come up with the perfect answer and swore by it. His explanation irritated her and seemed contrived. Her minor irritation lingered for a few weeks and finally abated as the fuel for her ill feeling drained away.

The years filled with her scorecard ratings for Matthew had passed and she firmly decided to leave her old judgments behind and to accept Matthew's tendencies to embellish his image and exaggerate his achievements. She came to believe that Matthew had more character and substance than any other man who'd been in her life. She'd traveled to Matthew's home environment in San Francisco only once in all those years, making sure he had the burden of travel while she remained on her own turf. She could look back and appreciate the harsh lessons she'd learned. She wanted balance this time. She felt her acceptance and understanding grow each day.

She was simultaneously terrified, awed, and calmed by the epiphanies and realizations that came to her. Her awareness and dedication became the essence of her very breath. All she wanted was to express her appreciation and demonstrate her love.

In fact, she'd turned her back on Matthew, had walked away from him for Big B, thinking Barry was the Gallant Knight who would carry her off on the White Stallion to his Castle on the hill. She was grateful for all she'd experienced and seen through that adventure that ended in disappointment. She recognized, in retrospect, having left Matthew the way she had, had turned out to be the one true path back to him, back to the unconditional appreciation and adoration of him that had never existed before.

The imbalance that had always lived between Matthew and her had been a big contributor to how they came apart, to how she made the heartless choice to say good bye. She'd wanted a level playing field; she'd wanted to be with her equal; she'd wanted a true partner. She'd wanted total trust and respect. The lack of balance with Matthew had been clear. What she never saw was how much judgment and condescension she'd consumed, and then turned into, that made her blind, that gave her a distorted vision of the truth. What she never saw was how she'd breathed in and held onto insignificant pieces of the past as if her survival and identity were bound to their legitimacy.

As she became able to shed these weights of perception, she felt herself evolving. When at last she saw Matthew for what she believed to be his real self with his many magnificent attributes and ordinary insignificant flaws, she felt as if she'd come full circle. She felt she might be able to have another chance to demonstrate her new awareness and deep love.

Of course, by the time she'd traveled down her paths of recognition and appreciation, and reached out to open the door of reconciliation, Matthew had healed and moved on. It had been almost a year since they'd seen or been in contact with each other, when he agreed to meet with her in her apartment in New York.

And there he was, sitting on the couch in her living room, holding her and listening to her without a drop of anger. She was overcome with joy to be with him again and be able to express all the gratitude, contrition and new awareness in her heart. "I'm so sorry; so, so sorry."

The tears flowed and the words poured out. There was only affection and tenderness. She saw his love for her still there. She felt like she might explode from happiness. She also clearly recognized the work that would lie ahead.

They sat on that couch and talked and touched for three hours. She told him her whole heart. "I know you can look into my eyes and see I'm telling you the truth of my feelings and where I am right now. I also know there's such a long history behind us that carries very different messages from what my eyes are telling you today. I know it's about putting in the time. We have to live this new truth together. Each day will be a new day for me to show you how real what I'm telling you is."

He told her about the dying mandolin player he'd befriended to help the musician archive his music before his death and how, through his beautiful relationship with this man, he'd finally healed from their breakup and gotten outside of himself and his pain from losing her. "He taught me how to live; he taught me how to die."

He told her about the woman he was currently dating. He described a recent night when he'd arrived at the woman's house to find her in excruciating pain, suffering from horrible digestive anguish and refusing to let him take her to the hospital or get any medical help that weekend. Subsequently this woman had been diagnosed with a large inoperable pancreatic tumor and was scheduled for biopsy surgery to verify the exact make-up of the tumor and potential treatments that could be provided.

They shared everything. They reconnected more deeply than they'd ever been bonded in the past. It was hard to leave her apartment. It was hard to separate.

Walking down the hill together to Grand Central Station where he was taking the shuttle to Newark Airport to fly home to California, they remained wrapped around each other like twin trees that had grown intertwined and were inseparable. The spring sunshine felt so healing and the white blossoms flew down from the Bradford pear trees on Park Avenue like a lovely snow shower.

She was reminded of when she'd told him she would not see him or speak to him again until he'd told Tina he wanted a divorce. This was such a different point in time. She'd broken up with him and crushed his heart. She had to prove her steadfastness and devotion for him to trust her again. She had to accept his ongoing relationship with another woman because of the tumor, because Matthew and she had such a long painful history.

She wanted to prove her new truth to him. She wanted to be punished and cleansed for her wrongdoings. She wanted to make him know he could trust her. She wanted to show her unconditional love.

As they approached the shuttle stop near 42nd Street, she heard music floating in her head from a long forgotten song from Michel LeGrand's beautiful score from *The Umbrellas of Cherbourg*. Just like Catherine Deneuve had promised to wait for a thousand summers for her lover's return, she could feel a similar pledge forming to wait for Matthew. She told him, "If it takes forever, I will wait for you."

As he boarded the bus to the airport, with them still embracing and clinging to each other, she promised, "I'll let you buy me that tattoo." She'd always said if she ever got one, she would pay for it herself. She knew how much he'd wanted to give that to her; the tattoo would be one more permanent and tangible proof of her devotion, of her belonging to him. The pain she would have to endure to get it would be fitting poetic justice as well.

On the walk home, back up the hill alone, out of nowhere, a second song played in her ears. Bob Dylan's pledge filled her heart. She felt there was nothing that she wouldn't do to make Matthew feel her love.

Ten days later, back in San Francisco, the biopsy confirmed the tumor was, as suspected, advanced inoperable cancer. Matthew had been faithfully emailing and texting her back in New York since they'd said goodbye at Grand Central and she'd been craving to hear his voice again.

She'd spent Memorial Day weekend with Rita in Rhode Island and had just taken the exit from the NYS Thruway to head down 9W to her Upstate Sanctuary. When her car speakers announced, "You have an incoming call from Matthew cell." she pulled immediately into a strip mall parking lot alongside the road. "It's really bad," he moaned. "It's an extremely virulent strain of cancer and there's definitely no possibility of surgery. She's in amazingly good spirits and taking it much better than I am."

She saw there would be no easy road back to what she wanted with Matthew. She recognized she would have to pay big prices without guarantee of reward. She knew she would have to walk the talk. She was aware she would not get to have what she wanted just because she'd had her epiphanies and realizations.

The Artful Liar

She would be patient.
She would be compassionate.

She would wait.

With her full and loving heart, she wanted to do all of this.

Letting Go Messages

Balancing Act

She learned how important it is to:

- Feel self-worth and pride from your ability to take risks.

- Apologize for hurtful behavior through demonstration of commitment and dedication.

- Appreciate the value of doing the right thing, even when the outcomes are quite different from your intentions and desires.

- Know rebuilding a relationship takes courage, character, acceptance and compromise.

- Avoid jeopardizing long-held and cherished core beliefs.

Year of Bliss, Year of Pain
(2013-2014)

It felt like she was Don Quixote on a mission to fight the windmill. There was a romantic allure to proving herself to the man she'd judged harshly and kept at a distance for so many years. It felt justified she had to be hidden and a lesser priority in Matthew's life because of the immediacy of the approaching death of the cancer-doomed woman who knew nothing of her existence. There seemed to be legitimacy in the punishment of it. She'd been the one who'd said good bye to Matthew in an email. She experienced it as a noble and honorable quest to demonstrate how she could shed her past harsh criticisms and demands for Prince-Charming-Perfection while Matthew was providing care and support for a deathly-ill, innocent woman.

She saw the dying woman as a bigger-than-life higher penance she had to honor before Matthew could be totally hers again. She was full of unconditional love. She kept herself free of judgment. She wanted to prove how accepting and appreciative she'd become. She wanted to make love with Matthew through totally balanced mutual desire and pleasure. She wanted to give much more than she wanted to receive. She wanted to confirm herself. She wanted Matthew to see her new truth. She wanted to show all of this to Matthew. It was a perfect storm.

She poured out proof to him every single day. There were poems, letters, lyrics, emails, cards, texts, gifts, words – all demonstrating and proclaiming love and devotion beyond any expressions of feeling and adoration she'd ever shown him during the ten years they'd been together.

The demands and romanticism of it all were heightened as the months unfolded. In early June, just before Matthew had planned to come back to New York again to be with her, Matthew had a stroke, which permanently took the vision in his right eye. The threat of stroke, heart attack and death loomed over them, heightening their awareness of life's limited time allotment and adding greatly to their desire to be together again. When Matthew was recovered and able to come back to New York in July, all the ingredients for their passion and appreciation for each other were in full bloom. She was immeasurably grateful to be able to express and show to Matthew all of her newfound unconditional appreciation. She was happy beyond expression they could make love in such a mutual and total way. She was grateful for their intimate time together as equal lovers, as real partners. It was as if they'd been rewarded with pure lovemaking that felt like the very first time.

They were able to be together again in August for the Falcon Ridge Folk Festival and in September for their annual walk on 9/11, from Ground Zero to Union Square, which had extra significance since they'd missed doing it together the past year. She had a tattoo of a heart embedded on the inside of her left ankle – that Matthew bought for her – as a symbol of how deep and permanent her remorse for having hurt him and her renewed love for him were. Their time together was magnificent. Their connection was cemented and true. They declared eternal fidelity and commitment to a future together. They wrote and/or spoke every day. They shared their lives across the many miles between them. They spoke of and confirmed how they were reunited in love and devotion.

In October, Matthew had another stroke which fortunately did not involve any further loss of vision but he did have nerve tingling along the right side of his body and his speech seemed a little hesitant. He was hospitalized for three days for observation and testing. They discovered through MRI that Matthew had had an earlier undetected minor stroke that had gone unrecognized when it occurred.

Matthew slowly regained stamina. He continued to experience fatigue that robbed him of his ever-abundant energy and phenomenal ability to fill his schedule way beyond a normal person's capacity.

There were more tests and doctor visits aimed at evaluating, diagnosing, and prescribing ways to deal with and battle the potential of another stroke or heart attack. There was also the dying woman's progressive illness which became more and more demanding.

She and Matthew were able to have beautiful loving days and nights together in early January to celebrate the holidays and New Year. In February, Matthew came to New York for a major international week-long conference.

On the third night of the conference, there was a big banquet at The Waldorf Astoria Hotel. The Foundation that funded the agency where Matthew worked was hosting this fundraising event and Matthew had told her how sorry he was he couldn't bring her as a guest because the entry tickets were eight hundred dollars; he couldn't afford to buy one for her; the spouses and partners of the event planners and facilitators were not included and there were no free entries allowed. She understood, of course, but felt very sad to be separated from him in the evening and she also knew the event would be lovely. One of her favorite singers, Nora Jones, was going to be the featured star performer that night.

Matthew left her apartment around 4:30 PM in his tuxedo, looking especially handsome. He wanted to get to the Waldorf early to help with some of the setup and to make sure all of the technology and presentation decks were in order. Matthew was going to be introducing one of the keynote speakers that night. It was a big deal event and he always got very stressed if he was unable to have abundant prep time before making a speech.

She'd wrapped her arms around him in a big hug as he was leaving, "You look so handsome in your tux. It's been a while since I've seen you wear it."

Closing the door behind him, she thought how glad she was he'd stopped wearing a hairpiece ages ago. She remembered the first time she saw him in a tux; she'd wanted to rip that damn thing from his head. It was hard to believe how long it had taken him to tell her about it and how long she knew and never asked about it or put her hands in his hair when they were making love. She shook her head in disbelief, thinking, "Imagine a man wearing a toupee and going to bed with a woman and not taking it off… and not telling her! Well, that was long ago and in the past, thank goodness."

Around 6:00 PM she was surprised to see his phone number appear on her caller ID. He'd called to ask her how long it would take her to get dressed and get up to the Waldorf. One of the big donors he knew well and had been good friends with for years had arrived and let him know her son had gotten sick that afternoon and hadn't come in from Connecticut with her for the banquet as planned. Matthew told her on the phone, "Delta hasn't invited anyone to take Robert's place and would be delighted to have you use his ticket and join her at her table. She remembers meeting you at that event we attended in Palm Desert years ago. Do you remember her?"

"Of course I remember Delta. I can be there in forty-five minutes. This is fantastic. Please thank her for me. I'm looking forward to seeing her again."

She remembered Delta extremely well. She remembered exactly what Delta had said to Matthew and her that night in 2004, "You two look like lovebirds. It's so wonderful to see you so happy again, Matthew. I was worried you were going to be Mr. Glum for the rest of your life."

"Sitting with Delta and being with Matthew's colleagues from San Francisco is going to be quite interesting," she thought as she rushed upstairs to her closet to see what shape her black cocktail dress with the asymmetrical hemline was in. She hadn't worn it in a few years and was pleased that type of hemline was back in style. Fortunately, she'd had her hair cut the day before and Irma had blown it out much better than she could. She knew she would look exactly the way she wanted for this special evening. Her appearance would be even more striking after her walk up Park Avenue and through Grand Central Station as her cheeks reddened in the brisk and frosty February air. She could walk to The Waldorf in just over ten minutes. "Get a move on, girl!" she told herself as she ran up the stairs to change clothes and get ready.

As she emerged from the arched corridor at the northeast end of The Helmsley Building, she pondered what Delta knew about Matthew's and her break-up. She wondered what Delta and Matthew's colleagues knew about his relationship with the woman with the tumor. She realized she'd never met any of Matthew's coworkers and didn't know anything about them. She didn't know if they knew anything about her. She'd been feeling so troubled and hidden lately. It was exciting to be going to a beautiful public event with Matthew. Validation and recognition were just what she craved.

Stepping off the curb at Forty-Ninth Street, she pulled her black leather glove up toward her left wrist so she could look at her watch. She was quite pleased to see she'd made it there before 6:50. Matthew was waiting for her at the main entrance to the hotel and immediately took her hand and walked with her across the lobby and up the escalators. "You're definitely the most beautiful woman here tonight. You look so pretty. It's good to see you all dressed up. I'm really glad this worked out like this. Delta is an angel."

She knew he would want to get ready for his introduction speech and she felt good he'd been there to meet her when she arrived and was still hanging out with her; she'd expected him to be too preoccupied with his responsibilities. He took the time to introduce her to several colleagues as they all moved through the silent auction corridor outside the Empire Banquet Hall where the banquet was taking place. He continued to hold her hand as they walked along together. She wrote in a $60 bid in the first slot on the bidding list for a tiny round Bulgari black ostrich-skin bag with a long cross body shoulder strap, knowing someone else was sure to outbid her for the precious cocktail purse. Its worth was listed at ten times her bid.

Matthew had just pointed her to where Delta's table was, way across the room, and kissed her on the cheek saying, "I'll see you after the dinner and speeches." when another work friend of Matthew's from San Francisco came up and greeted Matthew just as he turned to leave. The woman introduced herself, "Hi, I'm June. Do you live here in New York? How long have you known Matthew? How'd you two first meet?" June was very attractive with thick shoulder-length auburn hair and intense violet blue eyes; she was close to six feet tall. There was something very solid and bricklike about her that made quite a contrast to Matthew who'd looked miniaturized, slight and frail next to June. She amusingly pictured June with a cigar butt hanging from her lips. Matthew had quickly vanished and as she continued to soak up June's aura, the words "steamroller" and "ballsy" came into her mind. She saw and liked June's guilelessness right away even though there was something slightly invasive and uncomfortable about June's questions she didn't like. She answered June simply and succinctly, thinking there was an undercurrent to June's interrogation she couldn't put her finger on. Maybe, it was simply no one else she'd met that night had been quite as inquisitive … or was it as prying? …

When she would ask Matthew about June later on, he would tell her, "Oh, I've known June forever. We go way back. She's in P.R. and she asks everyone questions like that. Forget about her."

Her conversation with June came to an end rather quickly anyway because they were dimming the lights as a way to get people to be seated at their tables.

Walking along the geometric paths of the plush carpeting, she traversed the magnificent room with its three sparkling densely tiered massive golden chandeliers that somehow reminded her of a bizarre elaborate inverted version of a Kardashian wedding cake with hundreds of dripping candles. The cobalt and silver table cloths were glistening in the newly softened lighting along with the delicate gilded silver opera chairs encircling each table's circumference. There was a single shiny white pot containing a white multi-blossomed orchid plant carefully positioned in the center of each table. Delta had purchased six of the ten seats at Table 3 which was right next to the Steinway baby grand piano where Nora Jones would be performing. "Oh what a night this is going to be!" she thought. "Oh what a night this has been already!"

It had been so satisfying to have experienced herself as validated and coupled with Matthew. She hadn't realized how hungry she'd been feeling for such simple ordinary interactions with people in Matthew's life. She'd found herself squirming on a regular basis every day. She'd always pledged never to be in a relationship with someone who was in a relationship with someone else and here she was right in the middle of what she never wanted to do and be. She pleaded with herself to turn off these kinds of thoughts and enjoy the magnificent evening.

When she arrived at Table 3, Delta was there with open arms to greet her. She remembered how much she'd liked Delta who was a combination of opposites: tiny and tough, scrappy and elegant, streetwise and refined, filthy rich and down to earth. There was nothing pretty about Delta but her jewelry and clothes were the best money could buy, her taste was impeccable and she always looked sensational. If Delta knew any of the current components in Matthew's two-womaned life, there was no indication from anything Delta said or did that night.

Somewhere in the back of her mind she remembered something about Delta's husband being married to another woman when Delta and he were first a couple and something about Delta being pregnant at the time he was still married to the other woman, something about old school Catholic prohibition of divorce, something… Anyway, eventually Delta became the legal spouse and when her husband died, she'd inherited his millions. Delta probably wasn't the type to pass judgment on Matthew's and her situation but Delta's past was a likely contributor to an accepting and embracing demeanor. Delta asked no questions. A big contrast to June!

She decided she wouldn't ask Matthew any questions later about the details of Delta's past. He knew them, of course. She just didn't want to spoil the lovely glow she'd experienced being at the table with Delta and her guests, listening to Nora sing, feeling Matthew's shoulder against her own as they moved from table to table to chat with people at the end of the evening and to say good night.

When they both kissed Delta goodbye, thanking her again profusely, Matthew exclaimed; "Aren't I the lucky one, surrounded by the two most beautiful women here tonight!"

She and Matthew left The Waldorf holding hands once more and she felt so good to have had this public exposure, feeling like they were a couple, feeling like Matthew was totally comfortable being together with her and introducing her freely to everyone. She also felt delighted to be walking home with her new $60 Bulgari bag. Oh what a night!

In spite of the lingering glimmering residue from the night of the banquet, during the rest of that week she tried to speak with Matthew about how she was beginning to experience their relationship. She could feel Matthew closing down in his communications. After he went back to San Francisco, she wrote to him a few times pleading for openness and also asked him from time to time when they spoke to be forthcoming with her. It felt like he was withholding something. Each time she asked for openness, he told her the words would come. Each time she expressed what she was feeling, he acknowledged the legitimacy of her requests and emotions. Each time he told her he was blocked and unable to talk about his feelings. He said he loved her and he wanted that to be enough. He said, "I just want you to be all right."

She remained patient and understanding because:

- She'd been the one who'd hurt him so badly.
- There was an innocent woman with an advancing killer tumor who deserved protection.
- Matthew had endured three strokes and was under extreme duress and sickening stress.
- Matthew had told her he was not in love with the dying woman.
- Matthew had vowed if there'd been no tumor, he'd have broken up with the other woman, declaring his reconnection with the Love of his Life.

As time passed, it became harder and harder to be the hidden woman. She wanted a closeness and connection with Matthew that would make it feel right to be in a concealed relationship with him. She talked and wrote to him about what felt necessary for her to be able to get through it all and support him as this woman he cared about got sicker and died. Her friends kept telling her to avoid putting pressure on Matthew because of his extreme burdens.

Even Rita, who'd always had much disdain for Matthew, had pleaded with her to cut him some slack, "This guy is really under pressure. You've got to let go and let this play out. You can't expect any more from him with all he's up against."

Yet she kept feeling like something was really wrong, like something was being withheld, like Matthew was hiding stuff from her, like there was a bigger truth that was missing. She wrote him a wrenching letter about her struggles. He never acknowledged receiving it:

Matthew,

I'm going to try to write "IT ALL" succinctly and simply. First, let me say our love for each other is not in question! I see it as solid, deepening and unmovable. I know my continuing to fixate on what you're not telling me and what isn't being said is adding to your stress and I want to find a way to resolve this ongoing barrier. It's a vicious circle – quite different from FULL CIRCLE. Vicious and painful.

Each time I get to a place of acceptance and comfort, I end up with that tight constricting band around my chest and an empty-space, fist-pounding inside it. That's how I woke up again this morning. There has to be another way.

I know my own psychological baggage makes up a great deal of what I'm experiencing and that it's the case with you as well. Neither of us can fix that for the other nor is it what I'm seeking or asking from you. It's certainly the perfect storm from that perspective and we can recognize those elements that are in the mix and both of us can definitely grow and learn from these huge "particular" challenges we're in.

Along with the layers of psychological baggage that form a base for each of us, there are the ingredients of the triangle of deception and protection we've chosen to accept, to live. Yes, the foundation of TUMOR, CANCER, and IMMINENT DEATH have formed a very different reality from the one we would be in without those ingredients. And I recognize, along with the extreme pain for both of us, they have provided much benefit, enrichment, strengthening and learning. The truth is though, without them, I would never be in a hidden relationship with you while you're in a relationship with another woman. Yes, I would have tolerated a timeframe of duality for a period of time to rebuild trust and demonstrate the reality and substance of my love after such a painful estrangement and long history of incomplete love. Now it's a year out and you *cannot express to me what you're feeling and experiencing other than to tell me how much you love me (which I cherish). The truth is, even with the base reason of Cancer, I find it painful beyond measure that I am hidden and secondary, that you are living a dual life and that you are unable to be completely open with me about all you're going through and feeling. I know in my heart and in my gut and in my brain, if you were telling me your inner struggle and feelings, I could find a way to tolerate and accept this situation that has such basically unacceptable elements.*

I know little of what you actually feel. With or without intention or desire, your keeping all of this from me is a form of punishment and pain for me that makes this all impossible for me to tolerate.

I'm asking for words. I love getting the magnificent lyrics and the "oxox" at the end of your communications and hope you'll always send them to me; they mean so much. I just want your own words too and reassurances in addition to symbols and lyrics. These circumstances cry out for that. I cry out for that. I'm asking for total truth and openness. I'm asking for you to tell me everything. I'm asking for you to feel as much protection for me as you're feeling for her, without keeping anything from me.

Matthew, you know what you're feeling. Saying what you're feeling, facing what you're feeling, admitting what you're feeling seems to be where you're blocked, where you're choosing silence. Even if it's about protecting me or avoiding hurting me, I still want to know all of it.

Without your openness, I become the other woman; I become a second woman you're keeping the truth from. I really don't want to be that woman.

All my love is yours, always.

In one of their conversations about their struggle, Matthew responded to a question she asked him about the choice they'd made together to have a simultaneous intimate relationship that he was keeping secret from the dying woman. He'd answered, "I didn't know it was going to be this hard."

Early one morning in the middle of an attempt to have a serious conversation in bed, when Matthew was in New York for her birthday, she'd grabbed a piece of paper to write down a poem that had just slipped into her head:

what isn't said

what's wrong is
what isn't said

the way you hold it together
is by not talking about it

I can't hold it together
if we don't talk about it

what isn't said
tells me everything

She'd been pleading with him, "Matthew, please tell me what you're thinking and feeling."

"There's nothing there." he finally answered.

He was unable to speak or simply chose to stay silent. Within a few more weeks when he was back in San Francisco and she was in Virginia with family, she finally coerced him into giving her written words about their "situation". She'd written him she was word-starved and he'd emailed back he felt like he was forced to write. She read his words she'd hungered for, for so long.

Matthew had always been a gifted writer and fellow wordsmith. He'd always told her the way he processed everything was through the written word. When he finally responded in writing to her most recent outpouring, he avoided much of what she most wanted to know and crushed her heart with what he shared. She was stunned when he wrote of a specific promise he'd made to the dying woman he'd never labeled as a promise in that same way before. He attacked her tone of voice and her level of inquiry about the dying woman and wrote of the extreme pain and struggle he was experiencing:

> *I feel a headache coming on and am extremely tired today, but you are 'word starved' …. So I'll try.*
>
> *It feels to me you are misinterpreting so much of what I say to you. Each time we talk and I try to be more open, I hear the change in your tone of voice. I end up not wanting to tell you anything.*
>
> *Here's the reality I'm living with. First of all, she is dying and a cure is not possible. Secondly, I want her to have as much quality of life for as long as possible.*
>
> *You have asked me about my feelings for her. I do love her in a compassionate and enduring way. It doesn't change how I love you. Because she is dying, it makes love very different. She helped me get over losing you. The last thing I ever thought would happen was to have you come back to me.*
>
> *I want to be respectful of her, and it feels like I am violating her by sharing her situation with you.*
>
> *I see you as my safe haven where I don't have to talk about cancer and impending death. You want me to share everything with you about what's going on and tell you my feelings. It's just too much.*
>
> *You said you don't understand my extreme dedication to her. I made a promise to her when she got sick and I will not break that promise.*
>
> *I hate what this is doing to you. Dealing with two stressful realities is breaking my heart. Everywhere I turn, there is pain.*

It's starting to feel like I need to let you go to get rid of your pain until this is over. That way, at least one of us can be pain-free.

I know all of this is taking its toll on my health. You say you don't know how much longer you can keep doing this. I don't know how long I can either. I can feel myself losing ground every day.

I know it's just not enough right now. You want more than I can give. Each day is harder and harder to get through.

I apologize for not being able to give you more.

We are both hurting so much,

This is all I can write. I know it's not enough.

That evening, shortly after she read his words, she broke down sobbing in the arms of her dear friend Julie on the sidewalk in front of the restaurant in her Star City where they'd just had dinner. It wasn't so much from what he'd actually written. It was more from a deep awareness of how wrong everything had become. She wrote him a response, "Matthew, your words had a very deep impact for me. I want to look you in the eyes and talk - face to face. That's the only next step that works for me. Since "circumstances" prohibit my being in SF, let's work on making a time to be together and talk in New York as soon as you can make that happen."

She and Matthew continued to communicate by text and email but they stopped talking on the phone. Shortly after she returned to New York from Virginia while she and Matthew were still trying to get in-person time in New York on the calendar together, she had a reaction to some small details Matthew had written her about his involvement in an event taking place in San Francisco the next week.

He'd commented in an email, "I've been asked to emcee The American Cancer Society's Annual May Day fundraising luncheon next week on Thursday in partnership with KDFC, San Francisco's classical music radio station. I'm really excited I was able to get them a collection of Kevin's *Mandolin Musings* CDs to auction off. Kevin had such a huge following here in San Francisco and his widow Maria said she'd only want to donate the albums if I'd host the luncheon."

Her gut immediately whispered in her ear that Maria would never put an ultimatum like that on a donation. Matthew had never emceed this kind of event in the past; that role had always gone to a local media personality. Matthew was a frequent speaker in the not-for-profit fundraising world but he'd never had any media roles and he'd never been part of a charity auction. She figured he'd orchestrated and asked to be the emcee, using Kevin's mandolin albums as bait. It was like Matthew to exaggerate and inflate stories to make him look important and she had a nagging feeling that something was off in what Matthew had written her.

During the year of their reconciliation, she'd ignored other instances of this kind of exaggeration from Matthew. She'd come to understand it was Matthew's wounded self-worth that always made him expand stories and situations to impress people and she'd decided to overlook and even appreciate these types of behaviors. She knew where they came from. There was a little boy inside Matthew who needed validation and he'd figured out exactly how to get the ego boosts his inner child cried out for.

She knew it was also her own missing reinforcement from being a hidden secret woman in Matthew's life that contributed to the reemergence of her suspicions and yes, judgments. It was a bit like a dog that stumbled onto another dog's buried treasure: she felt like she *had* to "investigate" even though she knew that none of her concerns were a big deal.

"What difference does it make if they asked him or he asked them? How does it even matter if Maria gave the CDs with an ultimatum or simply donated them?" she admonished herself. "What the hell difference does it make?"

What stayed below the surface unarticulated, dominating her feelings, was how severely painful it was that once again, something of significance in Matthew's life, that she knew Matthew must have talked and bragged about to many people over what had to have been an extended period of time, had never been mentioned to her until the moment it was going to become public. "The American Cancer

Society doesn't plan, announce and roll out a public event over a ten-day period!" she repeatedly thought.

There were so many happenings Matthew had told her about at the moment they occurred or very close to that time. Or even afterwards. It was one of the main ingredients contributing to her feeling so disconnected and discontent. Things were popping up in Matthew's communications so close to the date of enactment. Certainly there had to be planning and discussion a long time before an event would occur.

It wasn't about the specific occurrence or the actual content of the situations. It was about the fact she knew nothing of them in advance and her input and support hadn't been sought or desired along the way. She was almost always uninformed about important happenings going on in Matthew's life. And then Boom! Out of the Blue! An American Cancer Society luncheon! Boom! The potential of a new cancer treatment. Boom! A head that was shaved. Boom! A trip to Vancouver for his dying girlfriend's family reunion!

Her intuition told her Matthew had kept everything about this luncheon out of his ongoing communications with her because it was a Cancer event. She suspected the woman with the tumor was going to be honored or included in some way at this luncheon. She ached with a sickening feeling of exclusion. She knew if she dared to comment on this communication omission, she would be admonished. She felt Matthew would come back at her with something like, "What in the world are you talking about? I told you I was going to host the luncheon. I'm not hiding anything from you. This is ridiculous, sweetheart."

She repeatedly told herself to "Let it go!" … and then finally decided to find a way to verify her suspicion.

Matthew's words the night of the banquet at The Waldorf kept sliding into her fixation. "Oh, I've known June forever. We go way back. She's in P.R. and she asks everyone questions like that. Forget about her."

She and June did not go way back. She'd only recently met June and their encounter had been brief. It was actually Matthew's own words about June that tipped the scales.

"We go way back."
"She asks everyone questions like that."
"Forget about her."

"Forget about her."
"Forget about her."
"Forget about her."

How risky yet necessary it felt to find a way to reach out to ask June a few simple questions. She felt disloyal. She felt compelled. She became a woman on a mission.

She didn't even know June's last name and she wasn't about to arouse suspicion by asking Matthew anything about June. She decided to see what Social Media would turn up. Matthew had hundreds of friends on Facebook …

It didn't take long to find herself on the phone with June. This time she was the one with the questions.

She was completely destroyed by what she heard coming from June's mouth. The American Cancer Society luncheon, Maria, and the mandolin CDs quickly disappeared in importance; it turned out what Matthew had told her concerning that event was basically the truth. She wanted to take back her call. She wanted it never to have happened. She wanted to un-know what June told her. The call left her cloaked in disbelief, like she'd been run over by a steamroller of denial while in her heart of hearts she knew every ballsy word June had spoken was steeped in the darkest truth she would ever hear.

As soon as she explained the reason she was calling, June blurted out, "I knew that night I met you this conversation was out there. I knew I couldn't keep being the front for a friend I'd lost all respect for. Somehow I knew you'd find a reason to reach out to me and I wouldn't be able to withhold the truth from you.

"You know you're not competing with a dying woman actually; you're competing with a tumor, with Cancer, itself. Have you seen the newsletters Matthew has created, written all of the content himself, and been sending to family and friends? You'd think he was the one who's battling cancer. The newsletters are full of comments like 'We are seeing a specialist this week to evaluate a new clinical trial.' and *'I've* discovered an alternative treatment protocol that *we're* excited about.' Everything is always about Matthew. I can send the newsletters to you if you haven't been on the mailing list. I'm not sure why I'm on the mailing list. I don't even know this woman.

"... I'm totally fed up with Matthew's exaggerated boasting. He knows exactly how I feel about his deceptions. I've told him over and over again.

"Matthew has been dicking around for years. He always told me how perfect it was you lived so far away. I'm not going to be his cover anymore. Just because my brother is one of his best friends and Matthew's always confided in me for some reason, doesn't mean I'm going to keep covering up shit for him like I always have. I'm tired of feeling dirty to protect him. I guess he's always thought of me as one of the guys."

The flooding, filth-filled history of deceit she found, instead of the misrepresentation of the luncheon, was shockingly unexpected and deadly devastating beyond repair. She was repulsed when she heard June describing Matthew's bragging about his exploits.

It seemed Matthew was full of secrets. She was struck by how much June knew about Matthew's past. She and Matthew had been a couple all those years and she'd never heard him mention June's name. If June hadn't introduced herself the night of the banquet at The Waldorf, this conversation would have never taken place.

The phone call with June led almost immediately to a call to Delta who was such a dear lady; Matthew had known Delta for many years and had been there for Delta when her husband died. She felt sure she would get disclaimers absolving Matthew if she called Delta.

What happened instead was the discovery of further incriminating evidence. Delta expanded on and reiterated much that June had told her. In contrast though, she did describe what a supportive friend Matthew had been, how easy he was to talk to when her husband had been so sick and died. Delta told her, "I always felt like I was talking to one of my girlfriends when I was with Matthew. Most men don't listen and share feelings the way Matthew does. And he sure could tell a dirty joke. We used to laugh together so hard my stomach muscles would ache from it the next day." She was stupefied hearing Delta talk about Matthew telling dirty jokes. She couldn't remember one dirty joke she'd ever heard from Matthew. What a different man she'd known from the one June and Delta had described to her!

There was even an incident Delta shared with her that was personally upsetting to Delta. Matthew had come to Delta desperate for money when he was getting his divorce and forced to sell his house. He was going to have some funds to invest for a few months after the sale of his house and before the finalization of the divorce settlement. He wanted to make a quick buck if possible. Delta had made an introduction for him with her financial advisor and Matthew took the advice he got from Delta's advisor and figured out a scheme to go around the broker to avoid paying him any commissions. "That really embarrassed me and I never felt the same about Matthew after that."

Even though she was hurting and drained from the call with Delta and had concerns about whether it was the right thing to do, she summoned the courage to call one of Matthew's daughters who was semi-estranged from Matthew but had stayed closely connected to her stepmom, Tina, after Matthew and Tina split up.

Matthew had given her Victoria's phone number shortly after his first stroke. She'd pleaded with him for it, "What if something terrible happened, something much worse, like a paralyzing stroke or heart attack, or God forbid, what if you died? Who would know to call me if something happened to you? Who even knows we're back together? I can't bear to think of something bad happening to you or your being hospitalized and I wouldn't know. Who in your life knows about us? Who could I call if I hadn't heard from you and didn't know why?"

For ten years she'd considered how much she wouldn't want to have to fly out to San Francisco if something happened to Matthew. She'd told herself it was about her fear of flying. Since 9/11, she'd flown as rarely as possible and almost solely for business, when there was absolutely no other travel option. She'd even taken the train to Montreal. Not flying to Matthew's sickbed or funeral was purely hypothetical, of course; she'd never been put to the test in their prior years together but it was definitely one of those shameful feelings that had brought her a good deal of guilt. She hadn't liked herself for being so indifferent and cold-hearted about this man she'd been dating and in an exclusive relationship with for many years.

It gave her a haunted feeling to know, as soon as they were reunited and she'd become one hundred percent committed to Matthew, he was in a relationship preventing her from jumping on a San Francisco-bound airplane to be his bedside partnered care mate.

"Who knows about us? Who could I call in an emergency, Matthew? Who would know to call me if something happened to you?"

"Victoria knows. Dan knows. I'll tell my cousin John because he always takes care of Frankie's food and kitty litter for me when I'm away. He's such a hermit who never says anything to anyone. And he is so loyal to me. He'd never tell anyone anything without me telling him it's okay. I'll give you all three of their phone numbers and I'll make sure they know to call you if anything happens where I can't be in touch with you, myself."

She got an eerie feeling when she called the number Matthew had given her for Victoria. "Good morning! Bay's Best Dry-Cleaning. How may I help you?" It was as if someone had slipped an ice cube down through her chest and into her heart; she had to swallow twice before the words would come out, "Sorry, wrong number." Had Matthew given her the wrong phone number for Victoria on purpose? She was starting to feel herself sliding down a steep slippery slope with absolutely nothing to grab onto and surely no way to change direction and head back uphill.

It was a bit embarrassing to call Delta back so quickly after their more-than-an-hour conversation. "Delta, is there any chance you know how I can speak with Victoria? Do you have her cell number or know how I can get it without setting off any warning alarms?"

Victoria's number had the same area code and the same last four digits as the number Matthew had given her but the other three numbers were totally different. ... Victoria was the only one of Matthew's two daughters she'd met. She'd been together with Victoria only once, the first year she'd known Matthew when Victoria had come to New York with her new husband to go to The U.S. Open Tennis Finals between Pete Sampras and Andre Agassi. She and Matthew had met Victoria and Darryl for brunch at The Boathouse in Central Park the morning before the match. The Boathouse was one of her much loved locales in New York, nestled in Central Park roughly a quarter mile away from bustling Fifth Avenue yet totally bucolic with old world quiet calm. From their table next to the windows, with Champagne Mimosas all around, she'd looked across the water and wished she still had her series tickets for the Open so she could be going to the tennis finals that afternoon too. She'd given up her subscription when the new stadium was built and the location of her seats and the price had both gone too high. She'd found Victoria a little standoffish that day but had never suspected anything underneath her cool demeanor.

To be having her first phone call with Victoria twelve years after the Boathouse brunch made her breathing shallow as if she had a hundred rubber bands wrapped around her chest. She'd turned into a sleuthing detective on the prowl searching for evidence, a spurned lover wanting revenge. "I'm happy you called," Victoria said, denying the sadness in her voice. "I had no idea you and Dad had reconnected. He was really bummed when you sent him that letter. He told everyone you had dumped him in an email like Berger dumped Carrie in *Sex and the City*.

"When he received that break-up letter from you, he'd already been pretty involved for a while with that woman from Sausalito who'd not been diagnosed with cancer yet. I didn't figure he'd stay heartbroken for long even though I knew he'd really loved you like crazy. He'd always bragged about your fabulous apartment and garden in New York, your house in the country and your work with all of the big networks and, of course, Oprah!

"You know, I'd always figured Dad must have painted a very different picture from what was going on with him and Tina when you and he first were seeing each other. I knew you were too far away to know the real story. And I knew Dad wouldn't want you to know what was really happening."

Victoria openly told her how Matthew's betrayal of Tina had nearly destroyed Victoria's relationship with her father. Victoria explained, "After all, Patty and I had already lost our first stepmom Lola when we were little girls. Lola had been away taking care of her sick father and had come back from Kentucky sooner than expected to find Dad screwing around with Lola's best friend Marta who was babysitting us while Lola was away. It was a nightmare! I think Dad thought we were too little to know what was going on but we knew exactly what had happened."

Victoria stopped talking for a few moments; she heard Victoria blowing her nose and then taking several long deep breaths before continuing, "That year was the worst Christmas I can remember. Lola came to be with us on Christmas morning when we opened our presents. It was one of those soupy San Francisco days when the fog never lifted. We begged her to come back home and stay with us and she told us how much she loved us but she couldn't be with our dad anymore."

She had an "Aha!" moment, stunned to hear Victoria talking about Matthew's involvement with Lola's best friend, remembering how strange she'd always thought it was that Matthew and Dan had remained such good friends when Dan was supposed to be the cause of Matthew's and Lola's divorce. Matthew's tears in Gramercy Tavern, when he'd told her about Lola and Dan, suddenly seemed pathetic to her; she'd felt such warmth for Matthew when he'd told her his version of that story. Suddenly, she felt like she was going to vomit.

There was something off-putting and uncomfortable about listening to a daughter expose her father. In spite of those distasteful feelings, she was grateful she'd made herself call Victoria. She appreciated Victoria's choosing to be so gracious after all these years of disconnection. Even though it felt like a sledge hammer had been taken to her solar plexus, she felt surprisingly liberated to hear all Victoria revealed. "It was so painful when Tina discovered all kinds of crap Dad had stashed around the house like cell phone bills, hotel statements and gift receipts. Every time Dad took a trip, Tina would go rummaging through his stuff, looking for evidence. And Dad just kept going with her to their marriage counseling sessions, denying everything."

Tina had confided many details of the couples therapy appointments to Victoria that summer after Tina got her doctorate. Tina complained to Victoria that it felt like Matthew and the therapist were in male-bonded collusion, making Tina out to be the delusional wife who imagined her husband was cheating on her. "Tina said Dad would sometimes just sit there in those sessions with a sick grin on his face, feverishly rubbing his head and saying nothing."

The icing on the poisonous cake being steadily built, layer by layer, with sickening gooey filling, came from Victoria's revelation, "In spite of Tina's determination to save their marriage and Dad's continuing to tell Tina, 'We can work this out, honey,' Tina was finally brave enough, after months of heart-shattering marriage counseling, to stand up one day in the middle of a session, throw down on the floor a gift and shipping receipt she'd found from We Are Erotica addressed to a woman in New York City … then walk to the door and with her hand on the doorknob, turn around and announce, 'Matthew, I want a divorce!'

"His lies of denial and her being the one who finally asked for the divorce almost killed Tina and even though I was *his* daughter, I couldn't take his side; I was devastated along with Tina. And Dad forced me to have brunch with you that time Darryl and I were in New York, remember? That was so uncomfortable.

"I think Patty has a bit of Dad's chemistry in her. She didn't even care what was going on when Dad started cheating on Tina and she barely communicates with Tina at all even though Tina is the one who helped so much with Patty's medical bills when Patty was so sick. Patty's also cheated on her husband with some dude at work for the last four years! …"

Listening to Victoria's outpourings, she was reminded of a New York City fire hydrant opened to provide relief on a sweltering August day with its gushing flow of water flooding over the curb and roaring down the street.

That third call to Victoria led her to a fourth call and then another call and still another. Her heart was in shreds by the time she finally got out of the path of the avalanche and stopped herself from gathering and corroborating any more of the dirt and damage she'd learned about Matthew.

Matthew was indeed the most artful liar she would ever know. The man who'd said, "I feel like I can tell you everything." had told her nothing, had immersed her blindfolded in his infinite pool of deception.

She communicated only two more times with Matthew via email:

EMAIL #1:

"I know everything. You are a sick man. I hope you get help. **When you told me you didn't feel worthy, I had no idea how worthless you were.**"

EMAIL #2:

"Matthew, given the givens, I can't see you in New York. I've learned a great deal of damaging and disturbing information which has torn me apart. At some point, I'll write more and/or arrange for us to talk. Please don't reach out or reply."

The days that followed were paralyzing. She found herself processing constantly. One day without leaving her bed, she wrote:

> *"I woke up this morning with the deepest sadness I've ever known. Like recovery from Novocain, it's as if the protective barrier of denial and numbness that accompanies the shock of trauma has finally worn off; I'm feeling Betrayal and Disgust in equal measure in their purest fullest capacity and depth.*
>
> *I'm overcome with overwhelming pervasive sadness that feels unending... I do not want to leave my bed.*
>
> *I will. I will get up. I will run. I will switch my winter and summer clothes. I will make calls. I will go on. I will survive. I will thrive.*
>
> *I will find my way back to joy.*
>
> *Damn Matthew Scudder to Hell!"*

She looked back at poems she'd written during the past year. Her breathing felt choppy and unsure as she read them and saw she must have always known much more than she allowed herself to acknowledge:

on the edge

she lives on the edge
where nothing can be solid
where pain and joy come in waves of paradox
and she is grateful for it all
knowing she feels in heightened senses
that make her more alive

the dripping rain tapping on metal outside her window
the whirling splash from the city's night traffic
the biting april air that stings the skin denying spring
the man on the plane who has left her again
to travel to the other coast
to fill his role as primary caregiver
for the woman dying of cancer
the woman who believes he is her true love mate

she finds her equilibrium
and takes her stand
she will not stay in duplicity
she will not live without openness
she will honor only truth

end to squirming

there is a point at which you cannot squirm any more
a set of circumstances where you can no longer be present
a place that feels too uncomfortable

there is a destination that requires truth without cover-up
a reckoning that demands nothing hidden
a heart rendering that eliminates duplicity

there is a home that welcomes your honesty
a mirror that helps you come clean
a sanctuary where safety follows confession

there is a trust that rivals all competitors
a doorstep where you are always welcome
a haven to enwrap you in solace

there is a point at which you cannot squirm any more
a set of circumstances where you can no longer be present
a place that feels too uncomfortable

deep inside

there is something deep inside that guides me
call it moral compass
call it soul
it declares whatever can be tolerated
it announces what is right

there is something wrapped around my heart
call it combatant
call it fear
it clings to crumbs
it settles for lesser priority

there is something painful that cannot be denied
call it cancer
call it innocence
it trumps my rights
it stomps on my emotions

there is something that i cannot shake
call it shield
call it blindness
it knows how close i feel to losing tolerance
it has no other place to go

there is something deep inside that guides me
call it moral compass
call it soul
it declares whatever can be tolerated
it announces what is right

Letting Go Messages

Year of Bliss, Year of Pain

She learned how important it is to:

- Refrain from feeling diminished because you believed and trusted a liar who betrayed your trust.

- Recognize lying is rarely directed at you, even when you're the recipient of the lies.

- See how deception is often about compensating for deep-seated neediness and insecurity.

- Know, even in your deepest pain, healing always comes.

- Honor truth above all else.

After Matthew

Hindsight Is 20/20
(2014)

There were so many ugly facts and repugnant behaviors she'd uncovered; she felt she couldn't face writing them out and seeing them in print. She didn't ever want to give Matthew a way to view the specifics she'd learned so he would know exactly what stories to fabricate to defend himself, thinking he could make the truth disappear by replacing it with his carefully crafted new rendition of it. She wanted also to protect her sources of information for the same reasons. She was determined to shield every resource she'd obtained information from. She'd seen his anger in the past and had also learned of physical harm he'd inflicted – something she would never have dreamt possible from the tender man she knew for so long and thought she knew so well. She didn't want to incur his wrath by disclosing such embarrassing and disgusting truths about him. He'd spent years hiding so much from her and making up elaborate stories to present such starkly different "truths" from the life he was actually living. He was exceedingly good at making up whatever he needed by inventing a background or supporting set of circumstance to camouflage reality.

She remembered as clearly as if they were happening right before her eyes and ears again – the first and last times she witnessed his ease and skill in deception and re-creation of reality. There was such an abundance of fabrication and invention to select from; Matthew was like a snake who could slither away in almost any direction, leaving you wondering if the truth you'd just seen had even existed. It always came to Matthew instantly to re-represent; he was gifted that way.

Neither the First Remembered Scenario nor the Last Remembered Scenario was particularly harmful or severely unethical. They just stood out in her mind, as the beginning and end of Matthew's "re-representations of reality." She had the same reaction both times, all those years ago and the last time they were together. Her gut went "uh-oh" in each instance. She felt there was something too effortless, too natural, too immediate in his construction of deception.

Another troubling element was how much pride he always took in his creation. She began to wonder if he'd ever had a guilty conscience or if his makeup was capable of human shame or repentance. It began to feel more and more creepy every time she thought about what would contribute to his effortlessness and then often denial of fabrication.

First Remembered Scenario (2002)

She'd flown up to Portland on Friday afternoon from L.A. where she'd been working all week, to meet Matthew for the weekend, before continuing home to New York on Monday morning. They were going to an outdoor concert to see Cheryl Wheeler and David Wilcox at Mount Tabor Park on Sunday.

She'd been able to add the third leg to her business trip at no additional cost. Even though she always insisted on direct flights to her destinations to reduce take-offs and landings which terrified her, she'd agreed to add an extra flight to her trip to meet Matthew on the West Coast. Matthew had been in Eugene at the University of Oregon for a Regional Conference: "Improving the Lives of At-Risk Youth." He'd driven the one hundred miles from Eugene to pick her up at the Portland Airport and then taken her to the Portland Japanese Gardens where the plantings were so lush she'd felt she'd been transported to Paradise. The soothing splendor of the koi ponds filled her with calm; she'd never seen so many of these beautiful colorful fish in one habitat nor seen any as big before. They were magnificent.

That afternoon Matthew was supposed to have attended a session back at the conference in Eugene – Sex Education in America: Lowering Teen Pregnancy and Drop-Out Rates – but he'd skipped out on the session to pick her up at the airport and spend the afternoon with her in Portland. His agency in San Francisco had set up a conference call at 5:30 PM for Matthew and three other members of the multi-disciplinary team who worked together to support and guide teenagers caught in the vast intricate workings of the San Francisco juvenile court system. All four of them, including Matthew, were supposed to give a brief report during the conference call on the session each had attended at different regional conferences. The Executive Director of Matthew's agency felt strongly everyone would benefit from hearing a quick debrief of the sessions that same day rather than wait until they could all meet together in San Francisco at the end of the month.

After they left the Japanese Gardens, Matthew had told her, "I'm taking you for a tour of downtown Portland. They say Union Station with its 150-foot-tall clock tower is a Portland landmark you have to see."

The train station, located at the foot of the Broadway Bridge in Old Town Chinatown, was indeed architecturally elegant with its charming Romanesque Revival tower, its shiny red roofing, and its "Go by Train" and "Union Station" memorable neon signs.

It turned out the reason Matthew actually wanted to go to Union Station was to be in a location that would replicate the sound of a conference center. He could make his call from Union Station and it would sound like he was calling from The Matthew Knight Arena in Eugene immediately following the session he'd just "attended." They found parking a few blocks away and had to run to get to the station in time for Matthew's 5:30 call. It was 5:27 when they walked through the main entrance. Inside the station, the ceiling's intricately carved wooden panels took her breath away and right in the middle of the station was warmly inviting Wilfs Restaurant with its piano bar and reputation for great jazz musicians.

Matthew whipped out the conference program as a guide, dialed into the conference call and there in the middle of Union Station, *reported on the session, including direct quotes from the speakers, questions he'd asked and comments he'd contributed during the Q&A at the end of the session. When the call ended, Matthew was grinning from ear to ear.*

Stunned, she asked him how he could quote the speakers and claim to have asked them questions when he hadn't even attended the session. He'd boastfully replied, "I had a conversation with each of the speakers at the opening session cocktail buffet on Wednesday night. I've heard all of them present several times and I'm proud to tell you I've read all their books as well. I could have made their presentations myself today but I'd rather have been with you and here we are.

"Valerie Day is performing at Wilfs tonight. I hear she's quite good. Shall we stay and have dinner here?"

She was dazed at how slickly and easily Matthew had orchestrated his contribution to the conference call. She could feel a strange sensation traveling through her body causing her to squeeze her eyes shut, shake her head ever-so-slightly from side to side and jiggle her shoulders, trying to make it go away.

She remembered that afternoon in Portland quite vividly. It was clear to her Matthew thought he'd impressed her by his deft cleverness and facility in depicting his presence at an event a hundred miles away. To her it had seemed deceptive and uncomfortable. It was the first time she'd felt that squirmy feeling she would come to experience with greater and greater frequency, particularly toward the end of the last year of reconnection with Matthew.

Last Remembered Scenario (2014)

It was the day before her birthday and her son J. had arranged a surprise to celebrate. Matthew and she were in her car and she was driving. She had the address but she didn't know the actual destination where they were going. She knew they were heading to Flushing Meadows Park in Queens and she knew there were many different venues there. Matthew had mentioned something about the Flushing Meadows Theater the day before so she thought she would be attending some kind of play or theatrical performance. She'd seen nothing advertised in Flushing Meadows Park so she really had no clue what they were going to see.

It was rainy and gray and the roads were messy and wet. The traffic was extremely heavy in the park; it was obvious there were multiple events going on. As she continued to follow her GPS to the exact address J. had given her, she saw she was circling Citi Field Stadium. She wasn't particularly happy, thinking she might be going to a baseball game. J.'s girlfriend's mother from Russia was in town and was to be included. The mother didn't speak English so an American baseball game could readily be a way to show off some American culture. But it was her *birthday and a baseball game certainly wouldn't be a choice she would have selected! A baseball game would be a huge surprise; that was for sure.*

She exclaimed in a clearly upset tone, "J. didn't get us tickets for a Mets game, did he?" Matthew immediately replied, "The Mets are very hot right now." She snapped back, "Damn, it's such a rainy night. I definitely would have dressed very differently if I'd known I was going to a baseball game. I sure don't want to sit outside in the rain and watch baseball tonight!" Again, Matthew was right there with a response, "There's indoor box seating, you know." She was feeling so disappointed and unhappy when suddenly the blue-and-yellow striped tents adjacent to the baseball stadium came into view and she immediately knew they were going to *Cirque du Soleil,* not to the Mets game!

As they entered the grand tent, she remained frustrated and annoyed at Matthew for his fabrications. She heard herself making puffs of air pop out of her mouth in disgust as she breathed. She silently brooded, "What is causing me to stay so upset with him?" He'd simply been prolonging the surprise for her. He had only good intention with his baseball comments. It was playful and good-spirited.

> *She felt angry about it anyway. It bothered her. It somehow felt connected to how easily and frequently Matthew had misrepresented something he was doing and she'd found out additional or hidden information or just questioned something about it in her gut. She kept feeling like he was hiding something from her or deceiving her. There it was: The Squirming! Her gut knew there was something wrong. Her gut knew she was being deceived. Her gut knew he was able to make up stuff on the spot, telling her one thing and then doing something different or hiding something else from her.*

She felt dirty and stupid when she realized how often he'd convinced her of what he wanted and needed her to believe. She knew many times whatever it was about was completely harmless. She also knew there was much harm within many of the deceptions and omissions Matthew had perpetrated and there was no safe route back to trust, back to belief. It was only about damage and loss now. It was only about letting go.

She stopped sleeping well as she dealt with her discoveries of Matthew's fraudulent behaviors. The healing came in gradual waves but very slowly. She'd held nothing back the year she'd just spent reunited with Matthew. She'd intended for this to be the "and they lived happily ever after" part of her life, finally. She'd been one hundred percent devoted and TRUE to Matthew during the past year.

As she started to come out of the inevitable stages of loss, she could feel herself letting go; she could feel herself getting in touch with her anger too. She'd always had a hard time embracing anger. She had a nasty sharp tongue when she needed it and could lash out with words. Her inner self resisted feeling any anger though and for the most part she suppressed it. One morning very early almost a month after she learned of Matthew's many transgressions, she woke up in a raging reverie of him.

Morning Dream:
> *She'd met Matthew at the Hudson train station. They were both so happy to be together and were full of each other as they walked down the street wrapped around one another. They were completely*

connected; their love was exceedingly strong and pure; it was also beautifully sensual and physical. They were so close, their bodies pressed alongside each other's as they walked, holding hands, their fingers intertwined.

Suddenly she came into reality and turned to him and glared piercingly into his eyes, exclaiming, "We can't do this anymore. We can't do this ever again. I'm furious at you! I'm so very furious at you for destroying our love. How could you do that? I'm furious at you for destroying us. I'm so furious at you! I'm so furious!"

She was intensely angry at him for his dishonesty, for the destruction of their love through his many horrible and hurtful choices and, most of all, for the dissolution of trust he had caused.

Letting Go Messages

Hindsight Is 20/20

She learned how important it is to:

- Recognize and avoid common pitfalls in life.

- Make sure those who want to have your trust have earned it.

- Be ready to cut losses completely when facing irrefutable proof of betrayal.

- Seek out confirmation and verification of discrepancies you feel suspicious about.

- Listen to what the dreams that wake you in the night are telling you.

Collusion with the Liar
(2014)

When you discover someone's been lying to you for years, it means you've been living a lie. You feel a kind of collusion with the liar. Somehow you know, even though your gut often told you something else, you *chose* to believe the lies. You feel dirty, like your very identity has been a lie. You've loved someone who isn't what he claims he is. She could feel herself not even wanting to breathe when she thought of how much she'd believed in Matthew, how she'd built and held onto truths about him that could no longer shine or be real.

She felt lost from her home bearings. She'd agreed to be hidden, to be a part of a grand falsehood. She'd come to feel devoured by deception as if she'd been slowly eaten by a monster, one mouthful at a time, one day at a time, leaving her feeling destroyed, detached and devoid of her true self.

As she fought each day to take in what his lies and omissions meant to her, she came to recognize he'd been more about deception than about what she'd cherished in him. The intersection of truth and fraud collided in her heart and her brain with such demand and immediacy that often after being awake for only a few hours, she found herself fatigued and desperate to crawl under the covers and close her eyes to hide in sleep.

The paradox of his fiery anger at how she'd broken up with him was astounding to her as she took in the years of deception she'd lived through with Matthew. It was hard to swallow. She felt sick when she thought of how she'd groveled the past year, of how she'd written him love poems of apology, fidelity and commitment, of how she'd promised to show him her true heart and devotion, of how she'd wiped the slate clean from all the events and behaviors that had legitimately brought out her judgment and rejection, of how she'd accepted his ongoing relationship with the woman with the tumor because of the way she'd broken up with Matthew and because of the innocence of this dying woman.

She felt appalled when she looked back at his discomfort and criticism about an email she'd sent him at the beginning of their reconnected year soon after the tumor biopsy, asking him questions about transparency. Matthew had proclaimed in an email, "My watchword is transparency. I am committed to being open and transparent with you."

Her email reply said, "Matthew, I treasure how committed you are to being completely transparent with me. That's the only way I can go down this path with you. I accept your desire to protect her from any more suffering than she's already facing. I still need to know how transparent you're being with her. What does she know about me, about our history, about our break-up? Who else knows we're reunited?"

He bristled at her questions, proclaiming her inquiry as too agonizing and weighty during this time of cancer diagnosis and support for the terminally ill woman. He'd declared, "I can't bear to read what you wrote or attempt to answer any of your questions about transparency at this distressing moment."

She backed off acceptingly, lovingly and remorsefully from her justifiable genuine inquiry. *Transparency* indeed! What right had he had to claim that word or complain about her natural questions when he'd never been fully transparent with her the entire time she'd known him! Looking back, she understood his ruffled reaction quite differently and could sense how intense that word must have been for him with his duplicitous hidden history.

She kept thinking about a conversation she had one crisp October evening with her good friend Paul Simpson, about two years into her relationship with Matthew. She'd just driven up from the City to the tiny Hudson Valley village where her country home was. She'd been away for a couple of weeks from "The Sanctuary" - the nickname she and Matthew had given the house that felt so endearing to her, similar to how she often called her precious little dog Bibi, "Monkey." Over the first year she'd owned the house, she'd made some lovely local friends;

Paul and his wife Carina had become dear to her. Paul and Carina had recently met Matthew when he was visiting from San Francisco; Matthew had gone with her to a big birthday party for Carina in early September. Paul and Carina had liked Matthew very much.

The fateful conversation that kept re-playing in her head had taken place a few weeks after the birthday party. She was out with a group of Paul's friends who walked or ran together and then all had dinner at The Blue Water Bistro on Thursdays. As she was walking and chatting with Paul and one of his friends, they started talking about Matthew; Paul had said to his running buddy, Michael, "You've got to meet Matthew. He's such a great guy. He's introduced me to some of the coolest musicians I'd never heard of before. You'll really like him."

She'd been listening appreciatively and commented, "Yep, you're right about Matthew; if you go to the dictionary and look up GOOD GUY, you'll find Matthew's picture there."

All these years later, after what she'd just learned about Matthew, she wanted to go back in time and be able to say to Paul instead, "If you go to the dictionary and look up DECEIVER, you'll find Matthew's picture there."

She remembered vividly how whenever Matthew would come to New York to be with her, he always wanted to spend as much time as possible Upstate in The Sanctuary. He would sit in the rocking chair with the leather cushions in front of the stone fireplace or in one of the rustic bentwood rockers on the front porch, gazing into space, lost in reverie. She'd always thought he was cherishing each moment there together with her. She'd felt he was demonstrating how connected he was to her life and showing her he was all hers.

She never could have imagined the Matthew who sat there rocking, during all those silent moments of deep thought, could have been pondering the juxtaposition of the two very different lives he was leading: the gentle tender elegant life he shared with her and the sordid duplicitous other life he kept hidden and undisclosed that had to be somewhere in his awareness, in spite of all they shared and all his declared dedication and loyalty to her and their sacred Sanctuary.

She knew the damage was irreparable. She knew Trust and Respect had been destroyed. She felt that even if Matthew could be mechanically and permanently "repaired" so it was both humanly and even robotically impossible for him ever to lie, omit truth, or deceive, she would still never believe him again, never believe in him again, never be able to trust him again. The words "Sadder than sad!" repeated over and over in her head.

She had to bury Matthew's loving tenderness just like she'd buried Jesse's spoons. She had to put away the compassion she felt for Matthew's tendencies that came from his troubled childhood.

What continued to torment her was how much she knew Matthew sincerely wanted to do the right thing even when his underlying intention was to build himself up to gain popularity, respect and acceptance. She recognized what a strong moral compass Matthew had, even when his choices were immoral. Matthew had always been the one she turned to for advice, support and good guidance whenever she was facing her own ethical dilemmas. He never failed to shine the light on the honorable ground for the choices she was facing.

She knew he would persist in telling himself he was a good person, that his deception was protective and helpful rather than face and admit his duplicity, fear, and need to revise history to his advantage. She saw his ability to reposition and reconfigure situations and actual facts to his benefit taking over to such an extent that they would become his new experience of his truth, of THE TRUTH as he knew it to be. She wanted to tell him, "If you hide the truth to protect someone from pain or to enhance how the person sees and appreciates you, *it's still deception.*"

Matthew had created a totally new life, a new world, a new identity for himself, the same way he'd become Matthew Scudder when he abandoned Samuel Matthew Scudder. On his twenty-first birthday he'd declared he didn't want to be called "Sam" any longer; he didn't like answering to his father's name when he had so little memory of his father and felt so little connection to him. A deeper and more likely reason was "Sam" felt too simple and plain for a man who wanted to be important to others, who wanted to forget the derision leveled against little Sammy Scudder. Matthew's business card, credit cards and work

Collusion with the Liar

ID said his name was Matthew Scudder. There was no longer an "S." there to indicate there'd ever been a Sam Scudder.

The biggest challenge was to reconcile all the facts that kept bombarding each other. The tenderness, adoration, dedication, and support she'd always received from Matthew made it challenging to take in and juxtapose the betrayal and dishonesty she'd uncovered. The two Matthews had to be joined into one person, into the man who'd lied to her. She had legitimate and multiple resources of information and tangible proof. The corroboration among those sources and in particular how the myriad of facts fit with or contrasted to the versions of them Matthew had shared with or exposed to her, made it CLEAR he had to stay eradicated from her brain and heart. Her friends, her family, her wonderful new therapist, all reflected back to her how imperative it was for her to eliminate Matthew from her present and from her future.

In whatever earlier ways they'd supported her relationship with Matthew and felt sympathy and understanding for Matthew's challenges because of his threatening strokes and his being with the woman dying of cancer, they all saw his sordid and longstanding deception as proof she had to give up any thoughts of reparation and acceptance. They all saw his behavior as sick and pathological.

Mostly she, herself, knew deep inside how critical and necessary it was to let go and put thoughts of and feelings for Matthew to rest forever. She needed to rid herself of his demanding presence in her mind. She needed to be able to drive her car, or walk up the hill from Third Avenue, or get ready for bed, without shouting aloud to the air, the street, or the bathroom mirror, "Liar! Lying bastard! Damn liar! Liar! Liar! Liar!"

The expression and experience of anger had always eluded her. She was good at guilt and sadness but had always felt anger was too primitive and raw for someone like her with her psychological awareness and emotional evolution.

Rita drove down from Rhode Island for a country weekend visit to lift her spirits and take her thoughts away from Matthew. At dinner, outside in the garden behind Hudson's Red Dot restaurant, she heatedly berated the server who had forgotten to bring the dressing on the side for the Cesar salad with grilled shrimp she and Rita were sharing. Rita gave her a reprimanding warning look from the corners of her eyes and she knew she'd made Rita uncomfortable by expressing her pent-up anger in such an inappropriate way. She profoundly and viscerally recognized how she was making herself suppress the rage, waiting to explode, somewhere in her inner recesses.

One day late in June, when she was finally switching out her summer clothes and moving her heavy dark winter wear to the back of storage and to the guestroom closet, she discovered a neglected business suit of Matthew's hidden way in the back of one of her closets. Matthew had asked her long ago to keep it for him so he wouldn't have to pack a suit for business meetings when he came to be with her in New York. She had no memory of it being there and she knew Matthew would no longer have a recollection of it either. He'd been bringing a blazer-type jacket on his trips over the years to wear with casual slacks to meetings. She couldn't remember when she'd seen him in a suit and tie other than the tuxedo he'd worn to the banquet back in February.

She pulled the dark gray worsted suit with its dusty shoulders from the closet. Matthew had always worn it with a crisp white dress shirt, gun-metal-colored cuff links and a green silk tie with dove gray diagonal stripes. The tie had brought out the subtle avocado-colored window-pane pattern in the charcoal wool and intensified the green flecks in Matthew's hazel eyes.

The first thing she did was lift the metal rod that had held the pants neatly creased and folded over the horizontal wooden cross-bar of the thick curved sturdy hanger. When she lifted off the pants, she saw a thread hanging from one of the pants legs and when she opened the pants flat to see where the string ended, she inadvertently pulled it until the entire hemline of that side was undone and hanging crooked, no longer sewn in place. She saw a small dark inky spot at the bottom of the zipper and when she placed her finger on it she realized it was a hole, probably from a moth. She let her fingers slide inside to examine the damage and suddenly found herself ripping the hole open further. When she saw how easily the fabric gave way, she grabbed each of the pants legs just below the crotch and yanked them in opposite directions as hard as she could and in moments Matthew's pants were in tatters and she was shrieking loudly and uncontrollably.

The fabric was old and threadbare in several places and easy to rend in any direction. She was liberated and horrified by the disturbing mixture of rage and glee she was experiencing.

Before attacking the jacket, she found herself checking the pockets to see if they were empty as if she were preparing to send the destroyed suit to the dry cleaner. From the inside jacket pocket positioned just over the left breast where Matthew had always put his wallet, she saw some fuzzy tendrils sticking out strangely. When she peered inside the pocket, she found Matthew's hairpiece, curled up like a sad little strawberry blond mouse that had crawled in there and died of starvation one winter. She wanted to flush the toupee down the toilet but was afraid she would pay the price later with plumbing challenges. She discovered when she pulled the two sections apart that were joined at the top of the center vent on the back of the jacket, the ease of destruction was available again. She'd never experienced such violent fury and its release was exhilarating and terrifying.

When she looked at the shredded pile of fabric that had been Matthew's once-beautiful business suit, her screams of joy and wrath turned into out-of-control peals of blasting laughter. She lay back on her bed laughing wildly, then slowly quieted herself and fell asleep in complete contentment.

The sky was fading to pink and the light was slowly leaving to mark the end of the day, when she woke up two hours later. She immediately got up and splashed some cold water on her face and then went down to the basement and opened the door to the trash compactor room where there was a thick roll of giant black garbage bags. She tore one off the roll and returned to her dressing room to gather the remnants of the suit, the evidence of her released hostility and ultimate joyful pleasure. She stuffed every last scrap of fabric into the bag, walked out to the corner of Madison Avenue and 36th Street with it and jammed the remains in the trash receptacle waiting there.

She'd kept the toupee so she would be able to take it Upstate and throw it off the Hudson River Rip Van Winkle Bridge she and Matthew had run across so many times together.

She knew time heals all wounds. She knew this would pass like all the other heartache life dishes out. She decided she needed to be less reactive and start taking initiative. She decided to make a list of all she'd cherished and believed most about Matthew and to make a second list of the lies and hidden secrets she'd learned that had ripped her apart.

She also set and wrote out the following goals:

- Seize and leverage my resilience.
- Write my heart.
- Come out of the discovery of deception as a bigger and better person.
- Make sure my story helps others deal with the deceivers in their lives.
- Trade my obsession for Matthew with the mission to tell my saga.
- Have an impact on the choices women make and on the way they get through and manage betrayal.

She was determined she would become stronger and smarter from her painful challenges and hardships and most of all, she would help others do the same.

Letting Go Messages

Collusion with the Liar

She learned how important it is to:

- Accept the pain that accompanies healing.

- Find outlets for your anger so you can be free.

- Make yourself clean through disassociation from deception.

- Seize the power you have to end obsession.

- Experience yourself as liberated and separate from the lies you believed and the dirty liar who spread them.

MAKING LISTS
(2014)

It didn't matter how many more lies and deceptions she could uncover. Everything he'd told her from the beginning had been based in fabrications and falsehoods. She knew figuring out how many more misrepresentations there were, or whether a particular element or statement Matthew had declared was false or actually true, was futile and self-defeating.

He'd often won her sympathy and acceptance for his exaggerations and inventions; she knew he'd suffered ridicule growing up fatherless and poor. She understood how he was always trying to fit in and be admired. It was astounding though how an awareness of some small comment Matthew had made would come to her and she could suddenly see how different the actual circumstance or true meaning had most likely been from what Matthew had claimed to be true to gain her belief and to win her love.

> *They were in the middle of a phone call and Matthew was telling her about two tickets to the upcoming Sandy Beaches Cruise with Delbert McClinton and Friends. He was telling her that the tickets were a gift from the siblings who wanted to give an extra special birthday present to their sister who was dying of cancer. The siblings wanted Matthew to go on the cruise with their sister; they felt she shouldn't be traveling unaccompanied. He said he'd told the siblings one of them would have to accompany their sister, as much as he'd always wanted to go on one of Delbert's cruises, he couldn't go. He described this to her on the phone, saying, 'There's no way I could go on that cruise; I would be too sick.'*

> *She'd inquired, rather baffled, "What do you mean, you'd be too sick?"*
>
> *Immediately, he'd replied, "Listening to Delbert and all of the music you and I love and share so deeply, I couldn't possibly go on that cruise with anyone but you. It would make me sick to be on that boat, listening to the music, looking out at the water and thinking of you the entire week. I told them there's no way I could go on that cruise."*
>
> *She felt comforted by his giving up this opportunity because of his love and loyalty to her. Delbert was how they'd met and the fact Matthew held that connection as sacred between them soothed her immensely. Knowing he was in the relationship with the other woman was difficult enough; the thought of Matthew traveling together with that woman on a Delbert McClinton Sandy Beaches Cruise would have been unbearable.*

It was almost laughable and even felt humiliating when she realized what Matthew had really been expressing when he'd first told her, "I would be too sick." She could feel the blood tingling beneath her temples when after she'd discovered Matthew's many betraying transgressions, she remembered a prior revealing episode that finally reminded her of the obvious reality underneath Matthew's words:

> *Paul and Matthew were big baseball fans and the two couples had decided to make a one-day excursion together to The Baseball Hall of Fame in Cooperstown. It was going to be a little over a two-hour trip and they set out at 9:00 in the morning for their drive through the fiery autumn landscape. They'd decided to travel north on State Route 81 for its back-road scenic country vistas; they'd be coming home after dark on the Interstate.*
>
> *When Paul and Carina picked up Matthew and her from the Sanctuary, Carina asked Matthew if he wanted to ride up front with Paul. Matthew climbed into the back of their Jeep Wrangler and said he'd be happy seated in the back with his sweetie.*

The subjects of their conversation in the car took as many directions as the curves in the road. As soon as they would return from a hairpin curve to the left, they would enter another to the right. At times all four of them would be sharing viewpoints on a single subject and at times Paul and Matthew were having a men-only conversation about baseball or stockcar racing while she and Carina got lost in gardening or fashion deliberations.

They were all talking about the announcement from the day before that Brazil had won the bid to host the 2016 summer Olympics and were fantasizing about how much fun it would be to go to Rio to see them together. She was looking over at Matthew as Paul said, "I'd sure like to see all those thonged bikinis on Ipanema beach." And Carina had quickly chimed in, "I bet you would!" She laughed at Paul and Carina as they ribbed each other in their usual playful way; she was picturing the photo magnet she remembered on Paul's and Carina's refrigerator with the row of bronzed Brazilian bottoms lined up on the beach – probably Ipanema. She saw Matthew was turning green and gasping for air. She privately whispered to Matthew while Paul and Carina carried on their good-humored taunts with each other up front, "Shall we ask Paul to pull over? You look like you're going to be sick." Matthew vehemently extended both open palms toward her as if he were trying to shove away the air between them and mouthed an angry "NO!" at her. She motioned for him to open his window which he did immediately.

She watched him turning greener by the moment. He was gulping and swallowing pathetically. She thought it was ridiculous that Matthew was too embarrassed to ask Paul to pull over and she knew it was only a matter of time before there would be vomit blown across the back seat from the open window next to where Matthew was leaning his woozy head. As they rounded another extreme curve, she shouted, "Paul, please pull over as quickly as you can; Matthew is going to be sick." The car was still in motion just before their screeching stop when Matthew tumbled out of the car with his morning omelet and sausage regurgitating from his heaving throat and mouth. She'd completely forgotten about what Matthew had told her about his motion sickness problems. He'd never been in the back seat when they were driving anywhere before. "This was so unnecessary." she said, shaking her head. "Carina asked you if you wanted to sit up front with Paul." She didn't feel particularly sympathetic since Matthew had known exactly what he was in for when he got in the car. Paul and Carina were compassionate enough without any additional empathy coming from her.

Matthew rode up front for the rest of the trip to Cooperstown and all the way home as well, even though it was Interstate, mostly straight and curve-less. None of them wanted to risk finding out how Matthew would fare in the backseat for highway driving.

It felt funny and painful when she finally put these two incidents together. "How had Matthew been able to turn on a dime when I asked him what he meant about being too sick to go on that cruise?" She realized when he'd initially made that comment, he'd been talking about his well-known motion sickness. The moment she'd indicated she hadn't connected his comment to his motion sickness and hadn't understood what he'd meant, he seized the opportunity to re-invent the comment into devotion and loyalty to her, "I couldn't possibly go on that cruise with anyone but you. It would make me sick to be on that boat, listening to the music, looking out at the water and thinking of you the entire week." He was a master of deception. It was astounding to recognize how gifted he was at this type of maneuvering. It felt Satanic to her.

She continued to see completely different sets of reasoning in contrast to many of Matthew's prior declarations. She saw a totally new basis for Matthew's always being the one who did all the traveling so she wouldn't have to fly which she hated, so they could be together Upstate in The Sanctuary which he loved, so she wouldn't have to be where his cats were since she was allergic to cats. June had told her Matthew had said he didn't want her to be in San Francisco because of his relationships with women and his ongoing dirty behaviors there; she could suddenly see a whole new set of motives that had never crossed her mind in the past.

There had been clues right in front of her all along. She could look back and see them easily, amazed to recognize how at the time they had stayed far from her radar screen, never entering her awareness. It reminded her of the Easter egg hunts she'd orchestrated for J. when he was little. He could always find the well-hidden and covered up eggs but often never noticed the ones right out in the open.

She was on the FDR Drive, heading north on her way to the country for the weekend. Matthew had wormed his way into her thoughts again. From out of nowhere, a conversation from another drive several years back started playing in her ears. They'd been on their way to Newark Airport. Matthew was having a hard time talking about an incident that had occurred several months before. She was concentrating on the route signs. She wanted to be sure not to miss I-24 East to I-78 East; if she missed that exit and ended up on I-78 West by mistake, Matthew would miss his plane by the time she could get herself re-routed in the right direction. She'd made that mistake the last time she took him to Newark; she didn't want to do it again.

She was trying to be patient, waiting for him to get whatever was bothering him off his chest. She hated how he would put off these conversations until the end of their time together; he would often bring up something difficult when she was driving and he was about to head back to San Francisco.

Matthew was talking about a session he'd just had with his shrink and finally blurted out, "Arthur said it's good, if you're sleeping with other men, that at least you're using a condom."

"WHAT ARE YOU TALKING ABOUT?!"

"Well, remember that time I was sneezing and we thought I was catching a cold? ... and you told me to go upstairs and look in your night table drawer because you kept Cold-Eeze in that flat box in the top drawer...?"

"Yeah ... and? ... go on... I don't have a clue where you're going with this."

"Well, you know ... I saw a condom in that drawer. It really upset me. I was very hurt, very, very hurt." After some rasping, harsh throat-clearing, "I never said anything to you about it then because I figured you hadn't realized you had condoms in that drawer when you told me to get the Cold-Eeze and you'd be uncomfortable I saw that you did."

"You've got to be kidding me! That ONE condom has been in that drawer for ages. I could've cared less you saw it there. I actually had no memory it was even there. How could you've made any assumptions like that just because there was a condom in my night table drawer? I went to a party with my cousin Richard when he was in New York on one of his buying trips. It was an AIDS benefit. They were raising awareness and promoting safe sex. It was a very elegant party and there were baskets and bowls of condoms everywhere. They handed them out to everyone as guests arrived.

"Matthew, you know I hate condoms. You know I'm not promiscuous. I'm pretty outraged you would even think for a moment I'm sleeping with anyone else. This is really upsetting me. Why in the world would you think I'm sleeping with other men just because you found ONE condom in my night table drawer? And what kept you from asking me right away if you were thinking that and if you were upset about it? None of this makes any sense to me. And HOW COULD YOU POSSIBLY THINK IT WOULD BE ALL RIGHT FOR ME TO SLEEP WITH OTHER MEN IF I WAS USING A CONDOM?!"

She'd felt like she might have some kind of road rage accident if she continued the conversation. Or that her head might explode. She'd made herself stop talking and stay calm so she could drive safely. She asked Matthew for silence.

When they arrived at Newark Airport, she pulled way ahead of the normal drop-off location so she could have a serious conversation with Matthew. She wanted to be away from the security guards who move everyone along the moment a car comes to a stop to drop someone off.

"Matthew, I don't want to be in a relationship with someone who doesn't trust me, with someone who doesn't know me well enough to know I have zero interest in playing around or having sex with someone else. If you think these kinds of things about me, I don't want to be in a relationship with you."

"Oh no, no, no! Of course I trust you. You know me; I was just so hurt. I'm sorry I upset you but I'm glad I finally said something. Let's forget all about it. It was a natural thing for me to think. I didn't have any way to know how that condom got in that drawer. Please don't be upset. Let's forget about this, please."

She had no idea how that long-ago conversation had spun into her mind so many years later. "How come I never questioned what HE was doing back then?" she asked herself as she drove across the George Washing Bridge, wishing her usual loving goodbye to the Empire State Building over her left shoulder and, as always, marveling that the big river down below rolling towards New York Harbor was the same sleepy, much narrower river that her little village Upstate rested against.

"How come I never suspected the reason Arthur talked to Matthew about my sleeping with other men was to point out to Matthew if HE was having sex with other women, I might be involved with other people too … and if so, at least I was having safe sex?" Those kinds of thoughts had never entered her head back in the day. As she drove north on the Palisades Parkway, with all of the damaging degradation piled up around Matthew, those kinds of clarifying, justifiable thoughts wouldn't leave her head.

Pondering what Matthew claimed Arthur had said about the condom brought her to a more recent conversation she'd had with Matthew involving Arthur. It had occurred soon after Matthew's second stroke when the demands of the cancer care and treatments were mounting exponentially and when she, herself, was starting to feel so much distress. She couldn't remember exactly where this talk had occurred but she had a vivid picture of the injured look on Matthew's face and could still hear the suffering in his voice after she'd said to him, "Matthew, I wish you would set up some appointments with Arthur. You haven't seen him in a few years, right? I know you've talked to a social worker at the hospital a couple of times but that just isn't enough. You're under so much pressure and I think you really need to talk to somebody professional and objective. I'm worried about you. Arthur always helped you so much in the past and it would be a lot easier than starting with someone new. And Arthur knows about our history so that would make it easier for you to share everything that's going on in your life right now. I really think this is important."

Matthew had looked like he was in acute physical pain, as if he were being tortured by an evil threatening tormentor. With that look of utter anguish on his face and, oddly for him, not even a hint of tears in his eyes, he replied,

"I can't go through all of that again with Arthur."

His response had an eerie tone she'd never heard coming from Matthew before. It was more animal-like than human, somewhere between a growl and a moan.

She said no more about Arthur after that. She was baffled and attributed Matthew's agony to all the pressure he was under. In her new awareness, she could only begin to think how much more Matthew's words — "all of that" — meant than she could have possibly imagined when he'd said them, back when she was innocent and ignorant of what was inside the unopened Pandora's Box.

Even though she was obsessed by the newly discovered shocking betrayal and dishonesty that had always been underneath the front Matthew had presented and by all of the disgust that had come out of her scrutiny and analysis, she made a commitment to write out a list of what she'd cherished about Matthew. It was therapeutic to set this goal and especially satisfying to realize, when she sat down to do it, there was little remaining she wanted to put on the list. It was strange and unsettling to sense the list would be brief and know at the same time some reflex component in her brain constantly held out hope her discovery was some kind of bizarre hoax.

There remained a demented desire deep inside her that the Matthew she'd believed in and loved for so long, and so devotedly the past year, would suddenly spring forth to declare his undying love for her and be able miraculously to erase his long history of lying and deceiving. Even with the abundance of undisputable evidence she'd acquired, it still sometimes felt impossible to take in fully that this man who'd been the center of her life for twelve years held no place at all for her anymore.

Matthew was the man she'd always wanted to talk to about politics and entertainment and literature and poetry. They'd been fellow wordsmiths together, writers and readers — poets — examining life and seeing the lilting beauty of the

Making Lists

written word, the magnificence of metaphor and the deeper "ethical" dilemmas in everyday occurrences. That would be what she would miss the most and have the hardest time understanding. She couldn't stop asking herself, "How could this man who has such a great moral compass and can always recognize and declare 'the right and ethical thing' to do, be the same man who lied to me and deceived me over and over again?"

They'd shared music in such a magical, meaningful and mutual way and she knew that would always be the link to Matthew that would hurt the most. All those artists and lyrics were woven into her core, into the fabric of her identity. Matthew had introduced her to Lucy Kaplansky, Chuck Brodsky, Jesse Winchester and many others. She'd sat in an iconic folk singer's kitchen while Matthew interviewed him about his troubled son's learning disabilities. She'd spent an afternoon speaking with a famous singer-songwriter and other musicians behind the scenes and at the sound-check for Levon Helm's Midnight Ramble that Matthew had gotten them two free impossible-to-obtain guest passes for from his friend Dan's brother who was a famous DJ in New Orleans. She'd been to Willie Nelson's "Hot Licks on a Cold Night" at Sundance with Willie's big black bus on view from their suite's bedroom window parked on the edge of the woods in the parking area right behind the lodge where they were staying.

And there was all the help and input Matthew had provided for her books, websites and marketing materials. Second only to her son, Matthew had been the one she always turned to for technology solutions. She'd liked that Matthew was so fully engaged in the current world and "with it."

When she thought about their intimate life together, her heart ached as if a dying ember would always smolder there to impede her breathing and cloud her desire for anyone else.

Once when they were making love, she hadn't been able to hold back her tears. She'd felt so sad, thinking of Matthew with the other woman even though he'd sworn there was no longer any sexual intimacy between them because of the advancing debilitating illness. "I can't bear to think of you with her. It hurts so much."

He assured her, "You mustn't ever have those feelings. With you, it's making love. It always has been. I was never making love with her; it was only sex. It always was only sex with her."

There'd been such tender passion, such connection, such loving sweetness between them. It was nearly impossible to cherish those memories now that she knew of Matthew's simultaneous sexual history and deceptions all those years. When she took in the knowledge of his perverted life, she was overcome by betrayal and a feeling of trust-stealing nausea.

The Dark that she'd come to know far outweighed The Light; she still forced herself to compile the list of what she'd cherished in Matthew:

The Light

- His playfulness and ease of engagement with people
- His participation and enjoyment in her favorite outdoor activities: tennis, skiing, hiking, biking …
- His politics, social awareness and world views
- His being well-informed and in today's world, culturally and technologically
- His passion for the music she loved
- His writing and word-gifted creativity
- His adventurous spirit
- His voice of insight, ethics and reason to help her find her way and make good decisions
- His tender and worshipful love-making
- His undying loving adoration he swore to give to her forever and always

And then there was The Dark, the unending list of what she'd often suspected in Matthew, augmented beyond her wildest imagination by the lies and deception that had sprung from Matthew's history when she inadvertently uncovered it. As the dishonesty and hidden parts of Matthew tumbled forth, she'd sought and found corroborating sources and evidence that proved, beyond any lingering doubt, his pathological lies and sociopathic behavior. Matthew's Dark list was irrefutable:

The Dark

- He had immediately broken his first promise she demanded of him never to lie to anyone.
- *He had lied to her.*
- He had hidden his involvement with other women from her.
- *He had lied to her.*
- He had participated in public sexual activity, bragging to people about it.
- *He had lied to her.*
- He had made up elaborate false explanations for unsavory, dishonorable and embarrassing activities.
- *He had lied to her.*
- He had advertised - and kept secret from her - his desire to meet women for romantic and sexual purposes.
- *He had lied to her.*
- He had repeatedly been involved in activities and then afterwards sworn to her a different description of what he had done.
- *He had lied to her.*
- He had used others in his life as excuses for inexcusable behavior.
- *He had lied to her.*
- He had kept many things from her, thinking she would have no way to learn about them.
- *He had lied to her.*
- He had claimed she was the love of his life and soulmate and then

chosen to keep significant information and behaviors hidden from her.

– *He had lied to her.*

– He had shared depictions of his history with her that were different from those he told others.

– *He had lied to her.*

– He had created enhanced revisions of his experiences and somehow convinced himself they were true.

– *He had lied to her.*

– He had presented more than one version of himself to the world and thought he could get away with it, that she would never learn he was living dual lives.

– *He had lied to her.*

It was a relief she could write out and see all of this in words on the page. As the declarations defaming Matthew formed in front of her eyes, it felt like she was crawling out from a deep dark hole, like she was purging the poison she'd unwillingly imbibed and pouring it onto stone tablets where it would be permanently etched as an eternal warning for her and the world to witness and stay forever protected from future exposure.

She could feel herself letting go, letting go of the Matthew she'd loved so dearly and could never trust again, and letting go of the sad sick man whose whole life had been built on deception, revisionism, and re-creation of the truth.

Letting Go Messages

Making Lists

She learned how important it is to:

- Write down the pluses and minuses of significant life challenges to support making informed and satisfying decisions.

- Look at every important situation from as many different perspectives as possible.

- Bolster choices by being aware of all that's happening without wearing blinders.

- Be trusting and truthful without becoming gullible and vengeful.

- Appreciate the good in others without blind acceptance of whatever they tell you.

Dirty Specifics/Big Lies/ Small Travesties
(The Proof)

She pondered long and hard whether to disclose the gruesome and dirty specifics of all she'd discovered about Matthew. She knew there was some eerie element inside her that still wanted to respect and protect him – and protect herself too. If she wrote it all and made it public she would look like a fool – and feel more like one than she already did – for having loved and believed such a deceitful man.

There was also the gratification she'd gained from her simple statement to Matthew when she abruptly ended their connection.

"I know everything."

It felt satisfying beyond imagination to keep Matthew in the dark like one of the bats hanging upside down in her barn with self-protective sonar to keep from bumping into anything in the night yet not really knowing what was out there in the darkness. She didn't want to give Matthew any way of finding out what she'd learned or how she'd obtained all her information. As she thought of the power this gave her, she breathed deeply into her gut and felt her clenched muscles letting go of tension.

Her fear of Matthew's wrath closely accompanied her sense of power; she was afraid he would viciously lash out at her and at the many others who'd exposed him to her.

She reflected on what she knew about the majority of abused women who return to or stay with their abusers out of fear, out of low self-esteem, out of familiarity, out of feeling this is what they deserve. She recognized she had to remove her fear of Matthew's fury from her deliberation and reasoning about whether and how much to reveal.

With these many wide-ranging pros and cons, she experienced and examined, an often repeated and fervently believed quote loomed into her consciousness:

> *"Heaven has no rage like love to hatred turned,*
> *Nor Hell a fury like a woman scorned."*
> (William Congreve, from *The Mourning Bride*)

Matthew had never scorned her but he certainly brought her shame; he'd deceived her and hidden his deceptions from her with brilliance. There could never be a deceiver more crafty and clever than Matthew. She wanted to avoid sounding like a whining bitch who'd been thrown to the curb; she didn't want to come across like a rejected woman who wanted vengeance.

Her feelings ran the gamut like the inside of a kaleidoscope with all the many broken pieces constantly changing their configuration. She told herself she had to think of her dilemma in a kaleidoscopic way. There was a myriad of patterns for her to examine and learn from. She wanted to appreciate and see beauty in her ability to break away from Matthew, to find benefit from what she'd gained from her loss and then to make good choices and move on with joy and radiance.

As she struggled and debated with herself on what specifically and how much to tell, she came in touch with her oath to share her story with other women to give them strength to be able to protect themselves by shedding deceivers and betrayers from their lives. It became clear that without disclosing the actual facts, she would fall short on this dedicated, promised goal. If she didn't share the specific details of how Matthew had deceived her, it would be simply generic, melodramatic, and even somewhat patronizing.

She'd come to accept that Matthew always liked to embellish and expand on what had actually happened, on how he told any story he repeated. She didn't like exaggeration or embellishment for any reason. She'd repeatedly told Matthew that. She told him often she never lied, never wanted to be lied to. Even something as simple as Matthew's using "best-selling" in a marketing flyer to describe one of her books had upset her. Matthew hadn't seemed to understand why that descriptor bothered her so much. By using that portrayal of her book, he'd claimed the exact public recognition she avidly wanted and in some venue in Matthew's mind, her book WAS a best-seller. She and Matthew would always disagree about this sort of misrepresentation.

She'd already identified and disclosed the first and last harmless examples describing when her stomach had twisted as she heard Matthew pull a made-up scenario out of thin air to hide reality. She'd already listed Matthew's Light and Dark sides in sweeping general definition. She finally decided to reveal Matthew's significant falsehoods she'd believed with scant questioning – even when her gut was at odds with her belief – **BIG LIES** he'd told her with over-arching effect, distinctly demonstrating why she could never trust or respect Matthew again.

She knew exposing Matthew's **BIG LIES** and putting them on hard, cold view was going to be like taking a scalpel and severing the invisible umbilical cord that somehow still kept her attached to Matthew, even after all the destruction he'd committed and all the exposure she'd already poured out. Before she could free herself completely, she had to honor and fully recognize the finality of her action. Laying bare the sordid details would mean there could never be a return to any form of reconnection with Matthew.

She knew revealing these dirty specifics would extinguish any spark of hope that might be hidden in her heart.

BIG LIE #1
*When Matthew promised her he would never lie to anyone ...

Soon after she first met Matthew, she asked him to promise her the reason for leaving his wife would be because he didn't want to be married to Tina any longer and not because he'd met and fallen in love with her. She also asked him to promise her he would never lie to anyone as he forged ahead on his path to divorce. He gave her these two promises with liquid ease, setting the stage for a deep and intimate coupled connection between them and simultaneously creating the platform of deception that twelve years later would annihilate all they would come to share.

"I promise you I will never lie to anyone. I abhor lying and the perpetrators of lies. You can always count on me to tell you the truth," he'd sworn to her.

BIG LIE #2
*****When Matthew reported to her he'd told his wife he wanted a divorce ...

Following Matthew's proclamation that he wanted to wait to ask for a divorce until his wife had attended her graduation and received her hard-won PhD, she told him she didn't want to be in touch with him in any way until after Tina's graduation, until after he'd told Tina he wanted a divorce.

It was stunning to learn all those years later, in addition to never ever telling Tina he wanted a divorce, that instead, he'd actually sworn to Tina he wanted to preserve their marriage, and claimed again and again to Tina there was no involvement with anyone else. He'd even proclaimed in writing to Tina, "We'll work this out, honey ..." swearing his desire to save their married life together.

What a shock to discover it was Tina who, after months of painful marriage counseling in which she was made to feel like a crazy woman who'd imagined her husband was cheating on her, eventually asked Matthew for a divorce when she finally found enough tangible proof of his unfaithfulness.

BIG LIE #3
*****When Matthew told her the only possible way he could have been exposed to and given her an STD was ...

As soon as she and Matthew moved into an intimate relationship, she was disturbingly diagnosed with a Sexually Transmitted Disease. "This is Doctor LaPierre; I got your lab report back this morning. It's confirmed. You've got gonorrhea."

Fortunately, she was alone in a private office behind closed doors, sitting at a desk in Burbank, looking out on the Verdugo Mountain range when she picked up and returned Dr. LaPierre's message to please call her back as soon as possible. To hear the "G" word come out of her doctor's mouth informing her of the test results when she was working in California, was nauseating and shocking.

She'd thought she had an infection, not an STD. She'd never before had such a diagnosis and she was sick that the poetic, tender man had contaminated her, the man who'd claimed sixteen prior years of monogamy with the wife he was divorcing. It was disgusting!

On the telephone call to Matthew following her conversation with her doctor, Matthew was equally horrified and said, "There's absolutely no way this could be true. I've never had sexual relations outside of my marriage. And Tina and I haven't been together sexually or intimately for years. It must be a false positive lab report you've received!"

She countered his remarks assuredly with the substantial facts that she'd had a distinguishing symptom when she'd been examined by her doctor in New York, and that the doctor had sent her off on her trip with two potent prescriptions for antibiotics, one to be started right away and the other to be filled in California if her lab result was positive, along with the instruction, "You absolutely cannot touch a drop of alcohol while on this second antibiotic. It's extremely powerful and it will make you very sick, even if you just take a sip of something."

To be in California without being able to lift a glass of wine at dinner seemed like an unjust punishment to endure. It felt serious. She'd never had that kind of prescription before. The doctor surely had known exactly what the diagnosis was going to be and she, herself, knew there was no possibility the lab report was a false positive result. She had symptoms and pain. Matthew had given her her first and only Sexually Transmitted Disease.

Within a few hours, Matthew called her back with a story he'd suddenly recalled, "You know, I just remembered I attended a bachelor party for one of my co-workers about a month ago. I was the oldest guy there and it was pretty wild. There were lap-dancers and crazy booze; I mean it got really crazy. I've never been to anything like that in my life."

Matthew claimed one of the lap-dancers had put her mouth on his penis and so maybe that had been the cause of this horrible experience she was going through. He swore by his story with a combination of shameful remorse and adamant vehemence she'd believed.

"I'll get tested right away. I still believe your report must be false. I just can't imagine I've got anything or have given you anything."

She'd let him know that kind of public sexual exposure was repugnant to her even if it was only a one-time event for a supposedly innocent reason like a friend's bachelor party the night before a wedding.

Matthew would subsequently claim his own lab test had come out negative and even with no symptoms and a non-positive report, the doctor had put him on medication too because of his exposure to her.

Matthew would also proclaim his innocence by telling her he'd insisted on a second test that had also turned out negative, even though she'd pointed out to him that since he was already on antibiotics, the second test was irrelevant and she was 100% certain Matthew was the only possible source for her diagnosis. She made it super clear she hadn't been with anyone else for almost a year.

As a matter of ethics, even though the timing made it clear this was unrelated to Jesse, she decided to share this information with Jesse, whom she hadn't seen or been with since the death of her father nine months before the STD diagnosis.

Down the years, if this topic ever came up, Matthew always stood by his negative test results and what he considered her false-positive one. His "truth" would always be there was no STD and she'd had an infection of some type that was cured by antibiotics. She always glared at him whenever he took that position, saying exactly what she knew to be true about her diagnosis.

She was able to believe his story about the bachelor party since she'd learned, in an NPR report, STDs could be spread through oral contact. It *was possible* his story was true. Of course, her gut and her friends were highly suspicious of Matthew's story but he seemed like such a plain, vanilla, good guy with steadfast and traditional morals, so his story somehow stood.

Her female doctor spoke to her about how men lie when she'd told Dr. LaPierre Matthew's story a few weeks after she came home from California. She heard her doctor's statement as a generalization about men and didn't recognize her doctor was saying it was highly unlikely Matthew's story was true.

When she shockingly discovered twelve years later, through her multiple investigative phone calls, Matthew had frequented and actively participated in open sexual activities with strangers at sex clubs (before she even knew him and during the time they were together), she felt sick to her stomach.

Every time she remembered Matthew's words, "I've never had sexual relations outside of my marriage," she would think of Bill Clinton swearing, "I did not have sexual relations with that woman."

She couldn't stand the thought of the stench she'd been unknowingly a part of and exposed to. She learned, at the same time she discovered Matthew's history of deception, even though STDs can be orally transmitted, lap-dancers aren't allowed to put their hands or their mouths on any part of the person they're performing a lap dance for.

She reflected, "Go figure; if only I'd known that lap dancer hands-free/mouth-free fact back at the time of Matthew's brilliant dodging-the-bullet STD story!" But then what difference did it really make if the lap-dancer story were somehow true? Matthew was such an artful liar and had told so many lies and perpetrated so many deceptions, there was simply no place left to go.

BIG LIE #4
*When Matthew told her the reason for his debt and unpaid loans was his contributing to his daughter's medical expenses ...

During one of her business trips to L.A., Matthew had joined her there and they'd driven to San Diego for the weekend so she could meet Matthew's Aunt Marilyn who was like a mother to Matthew. When she and Matthew came out of the nursing home where Aunt Marilyn lived, her cell phone rang and she looked down to see an unknown phone number on her caller ID with a San Francisco area code. Since Matthew was the only person she knew from San Francisco, she automatically answered the call and heard a voice, which turned out to be Tina, lambasting her, "You can have him and all his debt and all the loans he hasn't paid. He's going to do the same thing to you he's doing to me!"

She was outraged Tina had found her phone number and had the nerve to call her when she was under the impression Matthew had told Tina several months' back he wanted a divorce. He'd claimed they were legally separated with their divorce officially in progress. She was repulsed to hear about Matthew's debt and loan payment evasion. Financial responsibility, paying off loans and avoiding debt were as important to her as openness and honesty.

She said not one word in reply to Tina and jammed the phone at Matthew, with Tina still in mid-sentence, raging.

She couldn't really tell what Matthew was saying to Tina as he walked behind a huge bougainvillea bush with his hand over his mouth, mumbling a few words and quickly getting off the call. When he walked back over to where she was waiting for him to unlock the rental car, he practically threw her phone back to her as if it had come directly out of a pot of boiling water. She was livid.

"Matthew, you know how I covet my privacy. You know I've never wanted to be involved with a married man or with an ex- or soon to be ex-wife. You know how I feel about debt, Matthew!" She was furious Tina had gained her phone number and had invaded her life. She was fuming.

They were on their way to meet dear friends of hers who lived in La Jolla for dinner and there was very little said in the car on their way to the restaurant. Getting through the meal civilly was quite a challenge and it was fortunate when they first arrived, she'd had a few moments alone with her friends to give them a brief heads-up about what had just happened. She was like ice to Matthew for the rest of the evening and on their drive to the airport the next morning she could barely look at him or speak. She was still irate from the prior night's phone call and all she wanted was to get away from Matthew.

Matthew begged her to absolve him from his sins. He was so sorry Tina had gotten his phone records and discovered her phone number. He had tears in his eyes when he declared to her his shame for having accumulated debt and avoided paying off loans because of his diverting all of his available money to his daughter's medical expenses. He claimed this was not at all his usual approach to money and that it was his daughter Patty's death-defying, horrific battle against lymphoma that had precipitated Matthew's financial woes.

She listened. She softened. She believed. She trusted. She returned to Matthew...

It was crushing and outrageous to learn years later that at the point in time when Tina made that phone call to her in San Diego, Matthew had never asked Tina for a divorce and even worse he'd been continuing to claim fidelity to Tina the entire time she and Matthew had been involved with each other. It was even more upsetting to learn Matthew had always had a history of debt and loan payment avoidance and he'd never paid one penny towards his daughter's medical expenses. Matthew had barely earned any money to be able to do so anyway. Tina, the step-mother, had been the one who earned most of the money in their family and who contributed to Patty's medical expenses and ensured Patty got the right doctor and treatment for her threatening illness.

BIG LIE #5
*When Matthew said he thought he'd told her what kind of surgery he'd had ...

and

BIG LIE #6
*When Matthew claimed that he was embarrassed and preferred to be private about his sexual life ...

As a result of the STD, she'd refused to be intimate with Matthew until they could each be tested for HIV which at that time required a six-month waiting period after potential exposure. She continued to spend time with Matthew with extremely limited physical involvement. By the time they both tested negative for HIV and had re-engaged intimately, it became very apparent Matthew had a significant erectile dysfunction issue.

Matthew claimed, of course, this had never been a problem in the past and he immediately began to seek medical advice for dealing with his challenge. He told her, "I really don't want to take Viagra."

He looked into vascular surgery to repair impaired blood vessels. He did a lot of research on penile implants. He eventually told her he'd decided to have "the surgery" and that's all he ever said to her about it. He told her his good friend Dan was going to fly to San Francisco to be with him in the hospital for the surgery and to be there when he came home. During the three weeks following that surgery, she ran every day for him since he had a fifteen-year running streak and wouldn't be allowed to run those first twenty-one days right after the surgery.

Soon after, when they were together again in New York, everything seemed totally normal and she was quite appreciative of the benefits the surgery had provided. Matthew never shared anything at all with her about any details of the surgery and she assumed the blood vessels had all been repaired providing normal functioning. At some point down the intimacy road when her hand felt something irregular, she assumed it was scar tissue from the surgery and refrained from touching that area altogether afterwards.

Years passed, and it remained a "don't ask, don't tell" situation with completely "normal functioning" in the bedroom. One night, alone in New York, she fell asleep on the couch in her den in front of the television. When she woke up in the middle of the night, there was a rerun of that day's *Oprah* show and there were five women on the dim screen in front of her talking about a man all five women thought they were having a monogamous relationship with. All of them had become HIV-positive from this man. She had an immediate and very strong reaction and went straight to her computer to investigate. Strangely, it wasn't the multiple simultaneous relationships the man was having with these women or the HIV-exposure he had infected them with that bothered her and resonated so strongly; it was the man's deception that struck a chord with her. Her gut told her Matthew had deceived her for six years into thinking he had simply had vascular surgery without ever saying a word to her about his penile implant.

At the time of the surgery, he'd never mentioned having a penile implant or told her anything about how it functioned or what its parts were. She must have always suspected something yet when she Googled "penile implant" in the middle of the night, she was stunned. She was almost completely breathless with her heart racing rapidly when the first thing she saw was a graphic depiction of all of the implanted parts, where they were located and how they worked. It was immediately obvious to her the "scar tissue" she'd always avoided touching turned out to be a pump. There was even a video of the actual surgery. It was an extremely disturbing way to uncover this information.

She wrote Matthew she'd discovered something very troubling and would need some time before she could even broach the subject with him to talk about it. She felt sick to have been in what she believed to be a long-term monogamous intimate relationship with Matthew without his having had a conversation with her of any type about this decision or including her in some way to find out how she felt about his choosing to have penile implant surgery.

She finally was calm enough to have a conversation with Matthew following her Google discovery and asked him plainly, "What kind of surgery did you have six years ago, Matthew?" He immediately replied, "I had penile implant surgery."

Matthew acted shocked when she said he'd never told her that. She described what she'd just discovered on the Internet. He claimed it was a very big deal for him to go through the surgery and that he'd been embarrassed to talk about it or show her how it worked and so that's why he'd never mentioned it or talked to her about the decision to get a penile implant. He said these types of things were very personal for him and that he wasn't like her. "Hell," he said, "you've even written a book about your breast surgery and your implants. I'm much more private than you are about my sexual health and my sexual activities."

He said he'd even kidded with her about it once because of his implant and her prophylactic bilateral breast removal and dual breast implants. She actually did remember his making a joke after passing a woman on Lexington Avenue who had huge fake boobs but she hadn't even understood the joke he was making about being "a member of the implant club" or something like that, which had made no sense to her.

As always, Matthew was convincing, endearing, and apologetic, once again sucking her into believing his innocence and honesty.

She was the one who needed to be embarrassed and ashamed she'd ever believed Matthew's proclamations of discomfort, humiliation, and need for privacy.

Here's the reality about Matthew's implant she finally learned:

- Tina accompanied Matthew to his doctor's visits and was present to learn about the implant and gain an actual demonstration of how it worked.
- Tina – not Dan – was at the hospital with Matthew at the time of the surgery and took him home afterwards.
- Matthew bragged about his penile implant and proclaimed how cool it was to have a constant erection at sex clubs.
- Matthew paraded his nudity publicly at sex clubs and nude runners' races.
- Matthew had a history of E.D. for years before he ever met her at B.B. King's in 2002.

Seven years after the original implant surgery, Matthew again let her stumble onto something shocking that he should definitely have told her as soon as he knew about it. His implant had become semi-dysfunctional, causing his penis to have a ballooned tumor-like extension along the side. She'd shrieked and recoiled from Matthew when she discovered it and was outraged he hadn't prepared her for that discovery by telling her ahead of time. He made up some kind of story about it not having been that noticeable prior to her discovery and he thought she might find it pleasurable.

"Oh, please, Matthew; give me a break. If you knew how uncomfortable it was for me to be with you without your telling me about your toupee all those years ago and then how upset I was without your ever talking to me about your penile implant when you first got it, how could you have thought for a moment even that it would be okay not to tell me about this strange deformity before there was the chance I would put my hand on it and freak out?"

Somehow though she eventually, *once again,* became a sympathetic believer in him and his dilemma that required Matthew to face implant replacement surgery which he claimed he never knew was a possible or likely requirement.

During the last year when she and Matthew reconnected after their 2012 break-up, Matthew walked around with a boner at all times. She was embarrassed about its noticeable protrusion and yet accepted it without saying a word to Matthew about how obvious and distasteful it looked because she thought he was leaving his penis erect to avoid wearing out the pump mechanism that might cause him to require having yet a third implant surgery. She'd dedicatedly decided to be totally unconditionally accepting of Matthew.

Looking back on that blind acceptance was embarrassing. It made her feel like a fool that she'd gone out running with Matthew in New York City with him in his floppy knit sweatpants with his erect penis clearly at attention. How could he have thought that was okay with all those ads she'd seen, and knew he had as well, that said, "For an erection that lasts more than four hours, call your doctor." Did he think no one would notice? Did he think everyone would notice? "What the hell DID he think?" she wondered. And she'd said not one word. "How could I have participated in that without saying, 'Matthew, I don't want to be seen with you walking around with a hard-on. It's disgusting!'"

She remembered that first week after he'd met her at her apartment when she'd asked him to take her back; he'd sent her a photo of Dan and him at Candlestick Park down on the field after a Jackson Browne concert they'd just attended. She'd forwarded the photo to Rita and asked, "Does it look like Matthew has an erection in this photo?" Rita had replied, "Well, it sure does look strange. It must be something to do with something funny with the way the seams in the crotch of his pants were made. It must be."

After finally learning of Matthew's many deceptions, she could look back at the history of Matthew's parading erections and want, from deep in her heart, to be able to take back all of that acceptance and understanding. It was bad enough that so many men were always touching their private parts publicly (and not just athletes and rappers) but to have been out in the world with a man who had a constant erection was just repulsive! It was as if, to feel like a man, he'd needed to walk around with a loaded and cocked gun in his pocket.

BIG LIE #7
*When Matthew claimed to her he would never go out socially with another woman, even just to dinner or a movie, because he wouldn't ever want to send out a message that he was available or interested in other women romantically or sexually ...

So which is the straw that breaks the BIG LIE camel's back in the story of The Artful Liar? Certainly enough has been revealed here already ... maybe too, too much. As outrageous as what has been disclosed is, the worst part is, from the very beginning of their relationship, during all the time Matthew was proclaiming she was the love of his life - the ONE he'd always waited for and adored, Matthew had always been involved with other women exactly like during that last year his constant erection was always on display. Matthew was forever presenting himself as eligible, looking for sexual and romantic connection. He shared and spoke openly of his sexual exploits, thinking no one would ever betray him to the woman he loved in New York. He must have known someday she would find out the truth. He must have known that risk on some level.

For many years while they were a committed couple, he had active online profiles on the Internet describing himself foremost as an honest and true poetry man, proclaiming his search for sex and romance with a special woman. He was actively prowling, through his online dating profiles, even after she'd come back to him swearing devotion and after he'd proclaimed his mutual desire to be with her forever and always, even after they'd reconnected deeply, even after he'd had two strokes and yes, even after, as a public speaker at that American Cancer Society luncheon, he'd broken down, sobbing his faithfulness to the dying woman surrounded by her family members and the many other people attending the fundraising event. She knew he'd been registered for online dating for a long time because she saw he'd listed Franklin and Eleanor as his two pet cats. He'd had to put Eleanor to sleep three years before they broke up, three years before she sent him the letter telling him she didn't want to do anything behind his back.

She knew if she would challenge him about the cats and how long he'd had an active online dating profile, he would quickly say something like, "I was never on OKCupid when we were together. I put my profile online when you broke up with me. The reason it said I had two cats was because of how appealing it sounded to have two cats named Franklin and Eleanor. Having one cat named Franklin wouldn't have made me sound as interesting." She could hear him saying that as clearly as she could hear the subway's mechanical warning voice in her head saying, "Stand clear of the closing doors, please."

When she finally stepped back and took a good look at all the history and all she'd discovered in the end, she realized she knew enough without a drop of the new factual exposing evidence she'd gathered. At the time when Matthew had first told her the dying woman in San Francisco knew absolutely nothing about his having been in a ten-year relationship with her in New York and didn't even know who she was or that she existed, something about that had seemed very odd and unlikely to her. It just had never rung true.

She vividly remembered Matthew's tear-filled eyes very soon after they first met in 2002 when he told her in great detail about his past loves the night she and Matthew had dinner together in Gramercy Tavern. He'd always talked about his prior wives openly and candidly ... if not always honestly. Matthew was forever telling stories over and over to win sympathy or to try to impress people. She felt there was no way Matthew would have refrained from sharing their story. He'd even told her he'd bitterly told his friends she'd dumped him in an email just like Berger dumped Carrie in The Post-It Note episode of Sex and the City. Victoria had also repeated that same line to her on that fatal phone call she'd had with Victoria.

Of course, Matthew had such a beautiful explanation for why he never spoke of his long-term girlfriend in New York to his "new" girlfriend in San Francisco who he said had "healed his broken heart;" he'd claimed that because he'd loved her so deeply all those years they were together, he wanted to keep her and their love story tucked safely away protected in his heart and didn't want to give even the least little spark of focus to her so he would be able to keep from rekindling the flame of love that had burned between them.

Come on! How had she ever fallen for such an unlikely story?

Looking back, it felt clear and apparent; the only reason he would never have shared any part of the story of his New York girlfriend who'd ended their relationship via email was that he was already in the relationship with the woman in Sausalito prior to his receiving that fateful letter when she broke up with him. Everything seemed so obvious, given what she knew about Matthew and what she'd learned about his duplicitous history.

No matter what version of reality could ever be ascertained to verify how far back the relationship with the dying woman had actually begun, there was such a grand parade of outrageous claims, farfetched explanations and sordid history that belief, trust, and respect had been completely and irretrievably obliterated.

Small Travesties: Matthew had always, always made up his truth to protect himself. There were simply endless examples she'd always suspected were false promises, lies, and deceptions. In addition to the many significant bigger misrepresentations she'd learned about through her recent discoveries, there were way too many little white lies or red flags she'd ignored or accepted as Matthew's naïve or childish perspective that in retrospect felt equally huge because of what they embodied in the grand scheme of Matthew's dishonesty and lack of fidelity.

Small Travesty #1

The Hairpiece:
From the day she met him, she'd been suspicious Matthew wore a hairpiece so she was careful never to put her fingers in his hair. When she gathered the courage to confront him about his toupee, ask him how he'd ever gone to bed with her without telling her about it, and encourage him to stop wearing it, he proclaimed, "In all the years Tina and I were married, I always wore my toupee to bed."

Ridiculous!

The most telling comment he'd made during that toupee confrontation was, "I thought women didn't like bald men." She'd let him know, "What women especially don't like is men who wear hairpieces!"

Dirty Specifics / BigLies / Small Travesties

She'd comforted him by telling him, "So many cool attractive guys are shaving their head these days." She realized all these years later that instead of soothing his concerns, she should have asked him, "Why would a monogamous man be worried about women being attracted to him?"

That conversation took place on an airplane flight from New York to L.A. and they were the last two passengers still seated on the plane long after landing, engrossed in conversation. As they walked through LAX with Matthew on his way to his boarding gate to San Francisco, leaving her in Los Angeles, he asked, "Will you wait right here a moment while I use the Men's Room?"

When he came out, two minutes later, he was sans toupee! His bald head was beautifully shaped and she gasped a deep breath, squealed for joy and threw her arms around his neck and placed her hands on his smooth scalp and kissed him. She thought it was beyond courageous for him to have done that, done that for her.

What she couldn't have had any idea of, as she waited at the luggage carousel, was Matthew had plenty of experience exposing his nakedness to strangers in sex clubs and probably had sought and felt that same kind of thrill and adrenalin rush frequently and routinely.

For several months, Matthew wore his hairpiece in San Francisco and went without it whenever he was with her in New York or elsewhere. On the following New Year's Eve, Matthew shaved his head and swore never to wear his toupee again.

Small Travesty #2
The Card:
Another small occurrence that told the big story: Matthew had claimed a beautiful card she'd received from Jesse and kept on her dresser in the back of an art book, had fallen out of the book and landed on the carpet open so that Matthew accidentally read the card, thinking it was his own handwriting.

What bull!
She'd opened the art book and dropped the card a thousand times and it was simply impossible to get that card to land on the floor open.

Impossible!

Gravity and the heavy fold in the card would prevent it every time. And Jesse's and Matthew's handwriting didn't even look like they were taught how to write on the same planet. She didn't even care Matthew had found and opened the card and read it. She wasn't hiding it. It was such a silly and stupid claim and he held on to it for his very existence just like the monogamy he'd claimed with Tina and the implausible story of the lap dancer at the bachelor party at the time of the "negative" lab result for the STD.

Really!

Small Travesty #3
　The Photo:
She knew if she had to pick one wound that cut the deepest from every heart wound she'd had to endure, she would pick the newsletter photo.

Matthew had told her on the phone one Thursday evening in March that his music buddy Sean had promised him a surprise that night. "Sean is taking me somewhere special as his guest. He won't tell me what it is."

The next day he said, "You won't believe where Sean took me last night. It was to see Jake Ellis at Bottom of the Hill. What a surprise that was! I didn't know Jake was here in San Francisco. As always, Jake said to give you a big hug and tell you hello. I'll send you the photo of Jake and me we took for you."

Jake Ellis was a dreamy-eyed folk singer with a head full of soft baby curls. His rough gravelly voice denied his delicate little-boy appearance. She and Matthew had been Jake's biggest fans since they first saw him in 2006, the year Jake had won "Best New Talent" at The Falcon Ridge Folk Festival. They'd eaten dinner with Jake before he performed one night at McCabe's in Santa Monica. She'd surprised Matthew for his birthday one year with tickets to see Jake perform at Caffè Lena in Saratoga. Whenever Jake was performing somewhere only one of them could attend, they would always send each other a picture taken with Jake after the performance.

The last time she'd seen Jake perform was the previous November, two nights before she was leaving for Berlin to deliver her two-week Communication Essentials course for Bayer Global Initiatives. Jake was performing at The Turning Point in Piermont, New York. She'd bought Jake's new CD that night and had Jake sign it for Matthew to send to him separately from the photo of Jake and her she attached to a text to Matthew, sent directly from The Turning Point. Jake had been their discovery together and they shared him with each other in an intimate, personal way.

June, Victoria, Delta, and others had all been forwarding Matthew's cancer update newsletters to her. Matthew had been sending them across the Internet like a shotgun blast to everyone he knew, ... well, almost everyone ... When she opened an old update from March 15, 2014, she had to blink hard several times to convince herself of what she was seeing. There was a photo of Jake Ellis dressed in black jeans and a bright red cowboy shirt with black embroidered stars on each shoulder and white pearl snap buttons down the front, with his blue and green stitched guitar strap across his chest, his guitar showing behind his back and his left arm around a short little woman wearing shiny purple-framed eyeglasses and a makeshift scarf turban on her obviously bald head, both of them grinning affectionately into the camera.

The caption Matthew had written under the photo read:

"I surprised my girl with tickets to see our favorite singer-songwriter, Jake Ellis, at Bottom of the Hill last night. That smile of hers next to Jake would melt the stars. Imagine! We had just come from a chemo session. She is amazing!"

When she looked at those two smiling faces, she could almost hear the sound of ice cracking on the pond where she used to skate when she was a young girl. She remembered that sound from her childhood and how she had skated as fast as she could to the frozen edge, terrified the surface would open up and she'd be pulled down to drown in the icy-cold water below.

The Photo would always win first place with a perfect score of 10, no matter how many deceptions she reviewed in her head, critiquing and rating them like a judge on one of those stupid reality TV shows like Dancing with the Stars.

Once he claimed something, it became Matthew's "TRUTH."

She came to see it all like addiction. Addiction to women, to sex, to the thrill of deception. It was like a tic in his brain that had to be satisfied. She saw he was a defective man with a troubled childhood. She knew he'd worked on making himself a better person. She knew he was dedicated to helping the down-and-outs in the world. She knew he was someone who had lots of compassion for people's struggles. She also knew he was a sick man, a pathological liar. She knew he had to remain in her past ... forever and always.

Deception is rotten and spreads, killing trust and respect in a path of scars that can only heal through grand spans of time and will still leave huge reminders, thankfully for years and years, to prevent a future alliance with or acceptance of any form of lying.

Letting Go Messages

Dirty Specifics/Big Lies/Small Travesties

She learned how important it is to:

- Act on facts in alliance with what's in your heart.

- Face the realities that emerge from deception.

- Challenge flaws in and substantiate realities for explanations with unlikely elements.

- Recognize repeating behavior and communication patterns that reveal questionable motives and probable cover-up.

- Listen carefully when multiple people sense something is substantially wrong that you've ignored as trivial or inconsequential.

Trusting Your Gut
(The Warning)

The one thing she'd absolutely learned was to trust her gut. Hearing what her intuition was telling her was as simple as breathing. She knew her intuition was like a fine-tuned instrument and it was important to listen to it. She wondered how she could teach others to use their gut, their intuition, to their advantage, to be able to gain more perspective and insight from what their intuition was telling them.

She'd studied and was trained in facilitating workshops and processing assessments using Jungian personality theory and the Myers Briggs Type Indicator which examined the role of intuition in how people take in information. She knew some people were more comfortable taking in information that was concrete and sensory. Those people wanted to be able to see, taste, feel, hear or smell something tangible, something definable. The sixth sense – the gut – comes from somewhere else altogether. It's about the intangible. It's about what can't be touched, tasted, smelled, heard, or seen.

One night when she first knew Matthew, they'd gone to see Woody Allen's latest movie, *Hollywood Ending*, at Lincoln Plaza Cinemas on Broadway between 62nd and 63rd Streets. They'd arrived just as the movie was beginning and the theater was filled almost to capacity. There were a few single seats scattered throughout the darkened theater near the back and some open seats way down in front where she would be very uncomfortable watching the movie. As they moved along the side aisle, she was able to make out two single empty seats. She whispered to Matthew, "Here, you can take this aisle seat and I'll grab the one three rows down."

The Artful Liar

During the movie, she'd turned around to see if he was laughing at and appreciating the same scenes as she was but it was too dark to make him out three rows back.

When the film was over, she immediately got up out of her seat to walk back to his and found the seat vacant and figured he'd left the theater quickly which seemed a bit strange to her. She found him outside sitting gloomily on one of the outdoor benches in the open air terrace area behind the theater. "What did you think of the movie? I loved it! Téa Leoni was so good." she declared, smiling excitedly. She always loved Woody's films.

"Well, I didn't see the movie. I've been sitting out here the whole time."

"You what?" she exclaimed, completely dumbfounded. She couldn't believe she was actually seeing tears in his eyes when he said, "I was very hurt you left me there in a single seat to go off and sit by yourself." Matthew told her he would never have chosen to watch the movie if they couldn't sit next to each other.

They'd walked a block or so as he continued to lament how agonizing it had been for him. They ended up sitting on a bench next to Central Park while she listened to him painfully tell her how she'd hurt his feelings terribly that night. She was totally flabbergasted and could hardly believe her ears or take a breath.

She'd actually held on to the edge of the park bench as tightly as she could because she could feel herself ready and wanting to run away from him. She wanted to flee. He told her he would have left the theater and forfeited the tickets if the manager of the theater wouldn't have allowed the tickets to be used at another time when they could sit side by side.

Her gut reaction was to get as far away from him as possible. His neediness and insecurity seemed pitiful and she sensed there was something deeply wounded and sadly vulnerable in Matthew for him to have had such a strong emotional and sensitive reaction to something as innocuous and innocent as sitting in a single seat in a heavily crowded theater where the lights were dimmed and the movie had already started.

"You've got to be kidding!" was all she could think.

Of course, he wasn't kidding and she hadn't run away from him. She'd listened and become sympathetic. She'd forced herself to refrain from such a harsh and strong judgment.

She'd made herself ignore her gut.

She watched Matthew work on his sensitivity and insecurity over the years. She'd seen him mature and become more secure. When she and Matthew got back together after their year of separation in 2012, she saw a huge difference in Matthew. He seemed to have evolved tremendously and she loved how invulnerable and strong he'd become.

Looking back, there were many times when she'd had reactions and concerns she'd never expressed or let herself explore more fully. The last year especially when they were reunited, when Matthew had had the strokes, when the woman with the tumor had gotten sicker and sicker, she'd promised herself she would be unconditionally accepting. She saw the extreme pressure Matthew was under. She knew how frightening and threatening it must have been for Matthew to be terrorized with the potential of having another stroke or heart attack. She couldn't begin to imagine the demands and suffering the dying woman's declining health and impending death were adding to Matthew's struggles.

All of these extreme circumstances contributed to her ignoring her gut which continued to cry out for attention. The amount of suffering she would experience, as the year progressed, at the denial of her gut, was astounding.

During that reconnected year with Matthew, she'd had two terrifying dreams, unlike any she'd ever experienced. They were vivid beyond the possibility of a dream, waking her from slumber into pure panic, providing sinister proof of darkness.

Night Terror #1
She was struggling to get away from a molesting demon, a horrifying attacking intruder. He was clawing violently at her neck, trying to

silence her, intending brutal harm. With all the strength she could summon, she was pulling his slashing fingers from her throat, yet could not make him stop.

She came out of this dream with her hands at her neck, barely able to catch her breath, lying there, alone in the moonless night.

The next morning, as she was washing her face, she felt a stinging sensation along her chin and neck. When she looked in the mirror, she saw the deep purple, bruised and scabbed, claw-marked evidence of her night terror. She'd inflicted physical wounds to herself in her sleep, a never before occurrence.

She'd taken a photo as witness to her self-destruction as if she needed a badge of honor as an award for the survival from her ordeal. Later, she'd attached the photo to a text and sent it to Matthew, writing, "I had a horrible dream last night. A man was attacking me and I was defending myself. I actually harmed myself in my sleep and have bruises and marks all over my neck. You're supposed to be paralyzed when you're dreaming so you can't hurt yourself. I've never had anything like that happen to me before. It was almost as scary as the dream itself."

Night Terror #2

She was starting to wake up from a dark and menacing dream. There was a figure near her bed ready to envelop her. He was wedged in the corner between the white whicker chair with all the decorative bed pillows piled on it and her cherished, antique, red wardrobe cabinet. There was nothing to distinguish who he was or what he looked like. He was simply a cloud of black shadow and smoke.

She sensed she was dreaming and woke herself up to evade her terror. She opened her eyes to see he was still there, taking on more reality than in her dream. She sprang from her bed to battle him, pounding on his chest, her fists smashing through his threatening evil darkness. Her screams were her only defense to make him disappear.

The next day Matthew called her from the courthouse where he was waiting to find out if an accused fourteen-year-old boy's trial had been moved to juvenile court. The boy had killed his mother's abusive, crack-addicted boyfriend. She told Matthew on the phone call, "I had another nightmare last night. It continued after I woke up; it was so real. I was terrified. My throat is raw from all the screaming I did. I'm glad I was in The Sanctuary and not in New York where my next-door neighbors would have surely called 911 from hearing me yelling like that."

When she awoke from these nightmares of icy horror, she'd never made any associations with Matthew. Her unconditional return to him had deadened her to his sorcery and blinded her to the web in which she was enmeshed. Her situation was screaming from her subconscious to wake her up to the depth of deception surrounding her. Her gut was submerged so deeply that her intuition had to cry out its warning from beneath her sleep.

The learning that emerged from the jumble of denying imbalance was profound. She pledged she would never again ignore her gut at the expense of her heart and soul. She would make it a goal to help others develop their ability to hear their intuition and find ways to act on what they learn from doing so.

Without finally listening to her gut, she would have never gone on the search to uncover the truth Matthew had been hiding from her for years. Her gut paved the road to illumination. She was grateful.

Letting Go Messages

Trusting Your Gut

She learned how important it is to:

- Pay attention to what your gut is telling you.

- Look beyond your judgmental perspectives to understand the warnings coming from your judgment.

- Refrain from feeling like you have to defend your intuition.

- Seek out the tangible evidence that supports your intangible suspicion.

- Avoid letting others convince you you're suffering from "imaginitis" – remember the old saying, "Where there's smoke, there's fire!"

Picking Up the Pieces: Reclaiming Hope
(The Future)

She wanted to envision the future and knew it would be good to set some goals and map out how to reach them. She knew she was free and no longer depressed or sad. If anything, she was truly appreciative of how much she'd learned and of what she'd shed. She'd come to understand the burden of Matthew and all he represented. The main concept that overlaid what Matthew had encompassed for her was simply DECEPTION. It blocked out everything else she felt about Matthew and she deeply hoped one day she would find a way to push aside the negative feelings so she could remember and treasure all she'd had with Matthew and loved about him.

Matthew and she had shared so much together and he'd inspired her as well as appreciated who she was and what she stood for. She felt like she might never trust again and mostly like she would never *want* to risk trusting a man ever again. In contrast, she felt herself softening as each day passed and felt her playfulness and smile returning little by little so perhaps her return to openness and trust were closer than she imagined.

It was beneficial after all she'd experienced over the last two years, to be on her own and feel content alone. Second only to her wordsmithing ability, her self-sufficiency was her next greatest asset and she knew her sense of being okay "flying solo" was powerful and positive as long as she didn't become reclusive, shut down, bitter, and cynical.

Often she laughed too hard at the expense of men. Sometimes she criticized someone way too harshly who was a pitiful substitute for the anger she still carried for the lies Matthew had told. She sought to breathe easy, let go, find forgiveness and feel indifference, all of which she knew were needed for her good mental health, her capacity to heal and her sense of well-being.

She could forgive Matthew. She could let go of her anger toward what he'd done. She knew he was a sick man who used his lies to build himself up. She saw, even though she was the recipient of his hurtful dishonesty, the lies were more about his need to lift his sense of self-worth as well as somehow also to punish and deprive himself as unworthy and undeserving. This was all speculation and she couldn't actually know if these concepts she had about Matthew were true. They felt exactly right and she sensed she understood his darkness and what drove him to deceive.

She did know the more she could understand that Matthew's lying and dishonesty were coming out of his sense of survival and were needed to feed his inner craving rather than being directed at her, the more quickly she could heal and be okay again. She would be fine without Matthew. She would be finer than ever before.

A phone call with Barry one evening was the impetus for a huge step forward. Barry and she had remained good friends as the story of her reconciliation with and then escape from Matthew unfolded. She was exceedingly grateful for Barry's appreciative, undemanding, caring support. In that conversation Barry told her about a big decision his son Randy had made. Barry had always described Randy as a wordsmith like she was and told her how Randy had written poetry in high school and college even though he'd been a football player and a big jock on campus. Randy was the father of a lively three-year-old son and his wife was expecting their second baby. Randy had been a successful trademark and patent attorney for eight years and had come to Barry to let him know he'd negotiated a deal with the senior partners in his law firm to cut his work schedule by fifty percent so he could devote serious time to writing.

When she heard this, she told Barry, "Hats off to Randy for great negotiating skills. He must really be a valued contributor to the firm if they're letting him do that. Law firms are notoriously unwilling to make those kinds of arrangements with their attorneys. Good for him!"

Picking Up the Pieces: Reclaiming Hope

Even though Randy was only thirty-four years old, he'd had a mid-life epiphany and felt like he'd missed his calling. He was compelled to reconfigure the structure of his work life so he could faithfully fan the flame burning inside him. Writing was his passion and he was making sure he was true to himself without shirking his responsibilities and obligations. He'd been thinking this plan out for a few years; he'd been saving money and had a solid budget to put this all in place.

Barry had asked her awhile back if he could share her books and poems with Randy and she had, of course, happily agreed. Barry told her, "Randy asked me to ask you about your writing. He wants to know your writing schedule. He asked how many pages or words you produce a day. What kind of work plan do you have?"

She'd published two books; one was a professional development guide and the second was a memoir. Marketing had eluded her and the sales had never matched the quality of the writing or the heights of the reviews. Her poetry had been her biggest passion though her poems had never been published or publicized.

Her writing was simply an organic part of her life, almost like breathing, except, unlike breathing, there were times when she didn't write at all. Discipline and planning had never been part of her lifestyle or even her career management. She'd always been a spontaneous, free spirit.

Laughing heartily, she responded to Barry's inquiry for Randy, "You know, Barry, I haven't written anything since I learned of Matthew's betrayal. I've just been dead in the water with my writing. I've been completely blocked or "off duty" for months. If that weren't the case, I still wouldn't have much of an answer for Randy. I hate the word 'plan' and I hate the word 'schedule' even more.

"I write when I write. Nighttime, really late, is when I'm most productive. I've always told people I have a California body clock but lately I've started calling myself Honolulu Girl!

"Tell Randy I really admire what he's doing but I can't be much help in the discipline department. I've been feeling so bad about neglecting my writing."

She hung up, realizing what an inspiration Randy was to her. It had sickened her to think how she'd abandoned what had always given her the greatest satisfaction, what had always fortified her.

Entrenched, her writer's block was resentful and put up a pretty good fight. In the end, she was able to quell the monster. "I'm going to do this!" "I can do this!" "Go away!" she told the demon.

Lovingly and firmly admonishing herself, she said aloud, "If Randy – at his age and point in life – can make that kind of commitment to writing, then I have to be true to my passion to write."

The next morning, she woke up and wrote a poem before she even got out of bed. The following day she wrote two more poems:

it takes time

they keep reminding me
it takes time
to heal from profound betrayal
from painful lies
from deep deception

they keep telling me
it takes time
to recover from losing trust
from feeling empty
from being numb

they keep reassuring me
it takes time
to return from enveloping disbelief
from cavernous cynicism
from crushing loss

they keep saying
it takes time
and i keep asking
when

another day

another day
i might have climbed a mountain
written a poem
reached a goal

another day
i might have touched someone's soul
solved a problem
cooked a meal

another day
i might have emptied a closet
thrown out old junk
discarded excess

another day
i might have called to gather needed resources
made an overdue appointment
ascertained important information

another day
of doing nothing
feeling stuck
being empty

oh well ...
tomorrow is
another day

When she sent the third of these three poems to Rita, Rita emailed back, "Do I have to be worried about this?"

Picking Up the Pieces: Reclaiming Hope

reviving hope

the cinder holds a shred of fire
glowing dimly in the recesses of memory
in the bottom of being
somewhere in a lost dream
hidden in hope and refusing to die

the solitary challenge beckons
to revive the flame
to breathe life into smoldering remnants
sharing light anew
bringing embers back to blaze

It was heartening to realize that Rita read this poem as a love revival poem for Matthew. She immediately responded to Rita:

"Here's the good news: I never thought of Matthew when I wrote **reviving hope**. It isn't a love poem.

"I'm thrilled to be writing poems again. It feels so good! It feels like me!"

June called and wanted to know how she was healing. June knew what the discovery of deception had done to her. June realized how much June had contributed to the pain of loss.

When June said, "There are fuckers everywhere and it's up to us to keep their dicks out of our brains," she laughed appreciatively at June's ever-charming crudeness. She shared her latest poem, **what remains**, with June, asking, "Isn't it amusing how differently we've each expressed the same thing in such a different way?"

what remains

what falls away and feels like losing
sets you free to see what matters

what grabs your heart and burns your insides
shines a light on valued lessons

what fills your night and takes your slumber
shows you meaning long neglected

what grabs your thoughts and stalls your progress
holds the key to what is precious

replacing what feels lost and stolen
with knowing and accepting now

letting go is all that matters
what remains is all you are

The flow never stopped after that. She wrote daily for endless hours. She often went to bed as the sun was coming over the horizon. She fell back in love with writing. She stopped feeling lonely.

She was determined the writing she was immersed in would be much more than simply cathartic. She wanted her writing to be her platform of solidarity, her link to the future. She wanted to bring hope and healing to others who had been betrayed and deceived. She wanted to unite with them so her belief in the good that comes out of adversity, pain, and loss could be divided and doubled through her connection with those who were traveling through similar challenges. She wanted to build bridges to self-worth and contentment that many could travel across and then multiply their well-being among many more. She wanted to pay it forward.

Letting Go Messages

Picking Up the Pieces: Reclaiming Hope

She learned how important it is to:

- Keep your heart open even when you feel betrayal has damaged your capacity to trust.

- Guard against the tendency to belittle and find fault to compensate for the anger you feel toward those who have deceived you.

- Share your insights with others to add to their ability to manage the dilemmas in their lives.

- Seek and give support, without judgment, from and to people facing similar challenges to yours.

- Join with others for camaraderie and community and avoid isolation, self-pity and shame.

Sanctuary Lost and Found Within
(The Solace)

Maggie, one of her dearest friends Upstate, decided their friendship no longer held the same value they'd shared together for years.

It was the second time she'd had a close friend pull away who'd been so like family to her and who she'd felt would always be faithful and present in her life. The anguish of what happened with Maggie tore through her heart. She knew it was another lesson reminding her we can only count on ourselves. For sure, she still had friends who were true, who would be there for her always and she for them. That Maggie would not be one of them contributed greatly to her pain and to her learning as well. She knew because of financial pressures she might have to give up The Sanctuary and felt like she could. There was nothing outside of herself that could represent the meaning of her life.

These losses reminded her of the David Wilcox song, "Farthest Shore," about losing everything through destructive fire, diving into the water and swimming to the farthest shore with all possessions gone, and still having all you need because all you ever really need is inside you. The lyrics came back to her and she repeated them over and over to give her strength and help her know she would be fine without Maggie, understand a house is just a house, and accept Matthew was gone and in the past too. The freedom of it all became clear and she gathered strength with each breath she took in her new awareness.

She'd written a poem as an outcome of all her learning that expressed a quite similar type of awareness to David Wilcox's "Farthest Shore":

illusion

safety is an illusion
      we create to live in calm

we build walls we think will keep us safe
      that cannot give protection

with nets below life's treacherous tightrope
      sure footing can be tricked

we look to others for protection
      and learn our quest is hollow

the only safety that we have
      comes true from deep within

She was astounded at how much better she felt and how she could breathe so much easier without Matthew in her life. She realized she'd been participating in duplicitous dishonesty. She recognized she'd felt dirty and deceitful. She saw she'd denied many of her basic beliefs about living the truth.

It was reassuring and gratifying to realize, within only three months from the revelation of deceit and the abrupt and final goodbye she'd sent to Matthew, she could feel so transformed, uplifted, and liberated.

Looking back at the end of that significant summer, she realized, simultaneous to her agonizing struggle and then magnificent renewal, there'd been another ongoing revealing battle she'd fought, been marked by, and finally conquered that paralleled and symbolized all she'd endured and painfully learned:

> *Purging the Poison*
> *The weeds had taken over. She'd neglected her precious flower, vegetable, and herb beds that fateful spring near the end of May when she stumbled into Matthew's deceptions. Memorial Day had always been the big planting day in her Upstate gardens. Even though it*

actually took three months over the summer for the weeds to become deeply embedded and strangling, it felt like they'd sprung up in a single instant, like an unexpected, impossible, tangled jungle that invaded overnight to overtake her peaceful cultivated manicured landscape. When she'd learned of Matthew's many years of secrets and lies, she let everything go. There'd been no place inside her that could find a way to weed, plant, or nourish a garden. She felt deprived and depleted and completely disinterested in this spring ritual she'd always been devoted to and adored. To rid the soil of invaders and till the dirt to make it ready for new growth, blossoms, and vegetation seemed as far from her desire and delivery as our moon is from Earth.

Each visit to her Upstate Sanctuary over the summer brought her little of the old comfort and protection she'd always experienced there. The loss of Maggie's friendship had changed everything in how she spent her time Upstate. Maggie had been her gardening sister. Every year when it was finally past the threat of overnight frost, they'd always driven the beautiful ride to Greenville together, taking in the magnificent views of the Catskills on their way to Storey's Nursery, and filled the trunk of her car with impatiens, basil, rosemary, chive, heirloom tomato, arugula, kale, and zucchini plants, along with the likes of Russian sage, yarrow, and sedum to add to the other established perennials in their well-tended prideful gardens. On their way home, she and Maggie would end up lost in conversation, sitting outside at a curbside picnic table in Freeport, eating fresh-made sandwiches and drinking lemonade from the corner general store not far from the spot on the Catskill Creek where, long before she bought her house in the country, she'd caught her first trout on a fly with an Adjust-a-Bubble lure on an ultra-light fishing rod and spinning reel.

She'd felt too drained and lost from the initial shock and troubling aftermath of the discovery of Matthew's duplicity and dishonesty. She watched the weeds multiplying in July and August and thought during each visit she would tackle them and then plant her vegetables and herbs. All she seemed able to do was watch the menacing weeds grow and complain about their density and voraciousness. The winter had been brutal and in addition to the weeds being so unbridled, she'd lost all of the strawberries, the sage and lavender, a big butterfly bush, the beautiful clematis that grew and bloomed on the railings of the front porch, and a large section of the nearby dwarf lilac bushes.

Her resistance to taking on the garden endured and the weeds thickened and became entrenched. As the summer days passed and deepened into August, she regained her sense of well-being, worked her way toward letting go of the damaging love for Matthew that had held her captive, and distanced herself from the severe betrayal she'd experienced. As she re-acquired her sense of self, her self-confidence, her independent spirit, and her self-sufficiency, she could feel the yearning to rid her gardens of weeds finally turn into full motivation. There was an unusual change of weather in mid to late August with pleasantly cool nights and daytime temperatures barely reaching 80 degrees and, best of all, almost no humidity – so unlike typical August weather – which aided enormously in her finally feeling able to attack the weeds.

One weekend she spent weeding the flower beds that ran along the front of the house, bringing decorum back to the hydrangeas, ferns, hostas, peonies, irises, and day lilies. She recognized she'd dealt with the flower beds that had the least amount of weed invasion first and left the really wild and overrun areas untouched. It was a good start and gave her a sense of renewed accomplishment as well as pride and pleasure to see this weed-free area re-emerge across the front of the house.

The next weekend she returned full of determination to undertake the serious weeds that had assaulted the remaining garden beds along the southeast side of the house. The weather remained ideal even into the afternoon for this backbreaking work and she spent three days wearing the same gardening clothes each day along with heavy buckskin work gloves and her favorite knee-high, green, rubber boots that had the frog eyes and mouth along the toe area of each boot. These were the kind of boots typically made for little kids in children's sizes only and she loved splashing around in the rain wearing them. She'd decided to wear them for weeding to protect her feet and legs in case she encountered snakes as she worked, never thinking of any other hazards she might come across among the dense growth that would surround her hard labor.

The weeds were so thick and their roots so tenaciously embedded, she frequently needed to use a shovel and struggled agonizingly to unearth the undesired plants and then finally make sure all of their roots were fully removed. Some of the weeds were as tall as she was with unbelievably deep roots, a center "trunk" as thick as a small tree, and stems and leaves covered in hundreds of sharp needles she imagined could successfully compete with porcupines.

In two of the beds she pulled out long thick vines she'd never seen before. There were lots of tall grass-type weeds intertwined together among various other kinds of wild plantings with their grip in the soil ferocious and quite surprising. The typical weeds she'd always encountered in her years of gardening had always been easy to pull free from the soil with their shallow root systems.

She was reminded of her nephew Justin when he was just eighteen months old and unbelievably and stubbornly strong. If he had a toy or something harmful in his grip that needed to be taken away from him, it had been impossible to open his grasp on whatever he was fiercely clutching. Back then, she'd laughed quite hard at his unbelievable baby strength and at the same time been infuriated she hadn't been strong enough to take whatever he was holding away from him.

The progress was painstakingly slow and her determination and patience were boundless. She took breaks and allowed herself rest periods to nap inside on the sun porch, call a friend to chat on the phone, or take nourishment from good food she'd prepared. To see *the dark rich soil emerge free of invasive unwanted plants gave her an enormous sense of cleansing fulfillment. It was as if by digging deep in the dirt and struggling with exceedingly hard-to-achieve and time-demanding challenges, she'd been able to cleanse herself of entrenched contamination and reclaim her life, returning her to her true identity. It was as if she'd been held prisoner by Matthew's dishonesty and she'd committed herself to demanding labor to earn and be able to truly appreciate her freedom.*

The afternoon before she left to drive back to the City, she bought sixteen mum plants with rusty golden yellow flowers to line the newly weeded beds and planted them along both sides of the entry path and along the front of the house as a testimony to her hard work and as a way to honor the empty fertile, newly-tilled earth when it was too late for brightly-blossoming annuals or vegetable-bearing plantings.

When she'd been toiling in the garden those three days, she'd taken off the long-sleeve shirt she'd initially worn in the cool morning air and done most of the work in a thin-strapped camisole top with her shoulders and arms completely exposed to the air and sun. She'd gotten a few scratches on her arms and thought she'd been bitten a couple of times by some tiny odd scarlet-colored winged bugs she couldn't identify.

In the week that followed her intense work, she traveled to Virginia on the Thursday before Labor Day weekend and saw, after she arrived, her bites and scratches were starting to look irritated and get inflamed. Each day revealed more inflammation and brought more itching. By Labor Day Monday, exactly one week after her last day of weeding, she was in agony and knew she needed to seek medical help. At Urgent Care, the doctor told her she'd been exposed to some type of poisonous weed and prescribed six days of prednisone pills and the highest strength possible cortisone cream to apply topically.

Every day for two more weeks, the fiery red splotches, the rows of bumps, the hard, raised welts and the oozing blisters would continue to appear in another location on her body. The worst of it was up and down her arms. The itching was excruciating. She'd never experienced anything like it. She tried to imagine how much worse it would have been without the strong medications that were prescribed and the antihistamines she took in addition – all of which she got little if any relief from. The only solutions to soothe the horrific itching and allow her intermittent restless sleep in the night were the plastic bottles she filled with water and placed in the freezer so she could keep their icy coldness against her raging skin. It would take more than four weeks for the serious itching to subside and for the dreadful dark marks to fade.

She learned she'd been exposed to poison sumac that emitted a venomous oil from every part of the plant living or dead including the roots and that the viciousness of exposure to even the tiniest drop of this oil could remain active on any type of surface or location it touched for years. She would have to wear thick rubber gloves using alcohol to clean every surface in the house she'd come in contact with; she'd have to double wash her dirty clothes, in hot water and strong bleach; she'd have to hose down her frog boots and the front porch; she'd have to dispose of the work gloves and the container she kept them in.

She'd have to make sure there was no way for her to be re-exposed to the poison that made her suffer so terribly.

Throughout this entire ugly painful ordeal she remained calm and accepting. Amazingly, it all felt exactly right. As hard as the weeding process itself had been, as awful as the skin lesions and itching had been, and as much work as the purification/elimination process required, she felt nothing less could have ever measured up to the level of poisonous deceit Matthew had exposed her to and the necessary healing and valuable learning that had come from it. The poison sumac exposure was certainly nothing she would have chosen to go through and yet she saw it as the accurate and meaningful, ritual embodiment of what she'd experienced and gained through Matthew's betrayal. She valued and appreciated its warning and the purging of poison it provided.

The Artful Liar

When there was the chill of Virginia fall in the morning air and the leaves were displaying their first hints of red and gold, she was back again visiting her mother in the Star City and met her longtime friend, Julie, for coffee.

Julie had been a concerned ally who'd seen Matthew's red flags all along. Julie had been one of the voices who'd always suspected the boyfriend with the penile implant, who lived 2,500 miles away, was putting that implant to use when he was in San Francisco.

Over cinnamon scones and fresh-brewed dark roasted coffee, she'd said to Julie how wonderful it felt to be free of Matthew and how grateful she was for everything she'd learned and experienced. She'd told Julie she was thrilled with how magnificently her wordsmithing ability had been inspired and revealed through the horrendous exposure to Matthew's deception.

She proclaimed, "I feel so grateful to Matthew that if I ever saw him again, I'd want to kiss his feet!" She quickly saw the need to calm and reassure Julie, whose facial expression had instantaneously turned into an apprehensive grimace. She swore to her protective friend there would never be any possibility of her ever actually kissing Matthew's feet. Julie was immediately relieved and leaned in across the table and declared, "Oh no! You'd never want to do that! You don't know where those feet have been!" And they laughed lovingly with warm abandon exactly as if they were still the two young schoolgirl friends they'd adoringly been so many years before.

How satisfyingly wonderful that laughter was, taking her back to the opening words she'd written about "The Artful Liar" what seemed like forever ago:

> "She knew one day she would look back and find lightness and be able to laugh about it all. She also knew it would take a great deal of healing for that to happen; it would take much thoughtful processing to gain enough understanding to find humor in this awful mess of deception; it would take time, lots and lots of time."

Letting Go Messages

Sanctuary Lost and Found Within

She learned how important it is to:

- Value your personal integrity when you experience loss and betrayal.

- Gather strength from within when facing exposure to contamination and venom.

- Hold onto your own moral compass when others leave you feeling rejected and empty.

- Know that who you are and the worth you hold are separate from any possession you may own or feat you may be able to accomplish.

- Shed the weight of having deceivers in your life.

Final Dream
(The Epilogue)

The setting is an old Catholic church located not far from The Presidio. It's a cool gray day with mist rolling in silently and intermittently like the last traces of smoke from a campfire that was extinguished hours ago and still has one last log that refuses to die out. There are about 50 people present including close family members. No celebrities or musicians are in attendance. It's a memorial service for Matthew who died following a brutal heart attack that struck him down and stole his breath while he was running on an unusually hot day in San Francisco when the temperature exceeded 90 degrees.

She and Tina, Matthew's most recent former wife, are sitting in the last pew at the back of the chapel. Their shoulders are touching and they're holding hands. No one else who is there that day can have the same type of bonds they share with each other and with Matthew whom they're saying good bye to almost as if they are one woman. The next day they'll be traveling together to Seattle for a Lucy Kaplansky concert and then go on to The San Juan Islands together, a trip each of them took at a different time, of course, with Matthew.

At the end of the service, she'll read the poem she wrote for her father when he died, **grief's paradox**, to all who are there paying their respects to Matthew. It won't be for Matthew or for the loss of Matthew that she'll read it. She'll read it for herself, as a grand release for the beauty of all she'd learned from the pain and healing she'd experienced. She'll read it for the loss of what she believed Matthew was all those years they were together and for the splendid life she and Matthew could have had together if he hadn't been The Artful Liar ... and yes, she'll read it for all the poetry they shared.

grief's paradox

my grief is a flooding river
engulfing your sweet departed soul
every tear a vessel of safe haven
harboring your precious past

my grief is the color of unnamed darkness
robbing me of your true light
blinding brightness also shines
illuminating beauty you have left behind

my grief is a granite boulder
crushing my heart's depths with memory of your love
still silken threaded wings encircle
lifting your presence higher and higher

my grief is an open wound
bleeding from your loss
while gentle salve spreads
healing from how you touched my life

my grief is the purest pain
imprisoning my heart with your eternal absence
yet brings the gift to set me free
rejoicing in your everlasting being

Grateful acknowledgment: Two wonderful women who are gifted writers guided me and inspired me tremendously, bringing my writing and *The Artful Liar* to a level I could have never achieved without them.

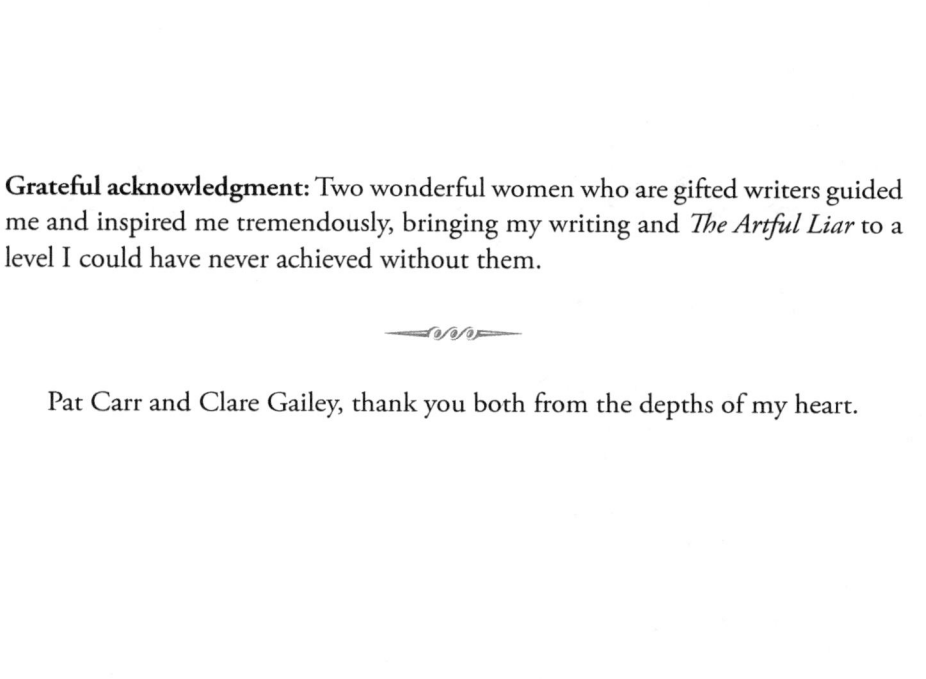

Pat Carr and Clare Gailey, thank you both from the depths of my heart.

www.ingramcontent.com/pod-product-compliance
Lightning Source LLC
Chambersburg PA
CBHW071731080526
44588CB00013B/1990